IDENTITY CRISIS
Finding Your Identity In Christ

IDENTITY CRISIS

IDENTITY CRISIS
Finding Your Identity In Christ

JENNIFER TODD-FLORA

Identity Crisis

Finding Your Identity in Christ
By Jennifer Todd-Flora

Copyright © 2014 By Jennifer Todd-Flora
All rights reserved.
This book or parts thereof may not be reproduced in any form, stored in a retrieval system, or transmitted in any form by any means- electronic, mechanical, photography, recording, or otherwise- without prior written permission of the author, except as provided by the United States of America copyright law.
First Printing, July 2014
All scripture quotations, unless otherwise indicated, are taken from the Holy Bible, New International Version®, NIV®. Copyright ©1973, 1978, 1984, 2011 by Biblica, Inc.™ Used by permission of Zondervan. All rights reserved worldwide. www.zondervan.com The "NIV" and "New International Version" are trademarks registered in the United States Patent and Trademark Office by Biblica, Inc.™other versions cited are Scripture quotations from THE MESSAGE. Copyright © by Eugene H. Peterson 1993, 1994, 1995, 1996, 2000, 2001, 2002. Used by permission of Tyndale House Publishers, Inc. The Holy Bible, New King James Version®. Copyright © 1982 by Thomas Nelson, Inc. All rights reserved
Copyright © 2014 Jennifer Todd-Flora

All rights reserved.

ISBN-13: 978-1500656034

ISBN-10: 1500656038

DEDICATION

For Nathanael, who showed me it's okay to let Jesus love me, who showed me my own Identity Crisis.

James 1:17

ACKNOWLEDGMENTS

I would like to thank my Mom and Bear for introducing me to my first Love, Jesus Christ. Thank you for doing your very best to raise me up in the Truth. Thank you for the mission trips, weeks at Bogg Springs, days waiting for me to get out of youth group. Thank you for the hours and hours of prayers. Thank you for maintaining your marriage, strong for fifty years.

Thank you to my amazing church, Shiloh Family Church. You are like a tall cold glass of unsweet ice tea with lemon in the middle of a hot Texas day. I am so proud to be part of this family.

Nathanael, Kim, Melody, Janie, Genesis, Diane, Mei, Timo, Justin, Esther, Samuel, Aaron, Scott, Heather, Audrey, Jeannie, Denise, Trish, Paul, Kricia, Lisa, Jesse, My Girl, Apes and Les, Senada and Mark, Ed and Geraldine, Mom and Dad Zink, Jason and Kristi - my love for you is deep and wide

My brothers and sisters in Love, Emma, with dimples as deep as oceans, Andi, Jeremy, Gage, T and V, Kristien, Nia, DeAndre, Lance, and all of those still on their way.
Jesus, my savior, my love. Holy Spirit, my best friend full of laughter. Papa God, You are good. I'll never doubt that again.

David, Karen, Janee, Marty, Naomi, Ann, Randy, Bonnie, Adam, Diane, Chris, Becky, Brandon, Josh, Ash

Thank you to Lisa Larson, my fantastic editor.

Thank you to every single one of you that have helped me not only move to Texas, but have helped me stay here. You know who you are, may God bless you exceedingly above all that you have given and provided for me, from moving my furniture, to helping with rent, to sending me purple goats in the mail. Your generosity and kindness is not over looked nor taken for granted. I love each one of you to the depths of who I am.

NTTD, and all those who have become new family.
Kiri Kiri

CONTENTS

1	Lawbreaker	1
2	Mirror, Mirror	19
3	Die Already	35
4	Love Slave	53
5	Adopted	75
6	Glue	89
7	Mind Control	103
8	Finished	119

PREFACE

I wrote this book for those of you who struggle to understand your worth, who you are in God. This is for those of you who don't understand how much Papa loves you. It is for those of you who have struggled under the weight of religion instead of being free in the beauty of Grace.

It is my heart that you will learn to look in the mirror and see the worth that makes God tremble with longing to know you. Lay down what you thought you knew, and come out of your Identity Crisis.

IDENTITY CRISIS

The more laws, the less justice

-Cicero

JENNIFER TODD-FLORA

1 LAW BREAKER

law·break·er NOUN \ˈlo-ˌbrā-kər\

: A person who does something that is not legal:
a person who breaks the law

I'm a lawbreaker and I'm not talking about the two tickets I've recently received for not wearing my seatbelt. The law is a hard thing to talk about. It seems to me that people don't want to accept full Grace because in many ways, the law seems easier. It's in our human nature to accept the free gift of salvation and put our own conditions on it, but Jesus didn't leave us with conditions.

Did you know that Jesus himself broke many of the laws of Israel?

He was an outlaw in so many ways! Before you throw the book away without even getting through the first page, hear me out. Jesus was perfect and without sin. He didn't break the Law of God. The Bible says He was perfect and without blemish, so how could He have broken laws and still have been perfect?

The law of man, the traditions, had been elevated to the point of being viewed as almost on the same level as God's Law in Jesus' time.

These were the traditions and laws that the Sadducees and the Pharisees gradually added to what God had given Moses during the forty years in the wilderness.

Here is why I bring this up. We have become a group of believers that are so convinced that we have to give God our fifteen minutes a day in prayer and quiet time, that we must attend church every Sunday. Individuals can't even agree as to when the Sabbath is to be observed. We are so convinced that we absolutely must tithe down to the penny of our income. Should that be our income before taxes or after? Please don't misunderstand me. I believe these things are all well and good. Beneficial even, but only when it comes out of a heart that is surrendered to the love of Jesus first and foremost.

I want us to take a good hard look at the character of Jesus. In that we find how God sees us. Stripped clean of all of the self-imposed regulations and just raw before Him. Does that scare you a little? Does it make your heart race to think that maybe, just maybe, God would still love you the very same if you gave up teaching that kindergarten Sunday School class that takes up all of your family time on Saturday night as you prepare? What if, God just wanted us, not our traditions and futile attempts to achieve righteousness. Let's go back to the very beginning of Jesus' entrance into Priesthood. Imagine Passover, and Mary and Joseph have traveled with Jesus, and I'm sure that the rest of the family to Jerusalem for the Passover Feast. When it was over, they start heading back to Nazareth. Jesus, wasn't with them. The best estimate that I've been able to find is that it's about a four days journey on foot. So there they are, already a day into their journey, and Jesus has gone missing. So panicked, I'm sure, they turn around walk another day's journey back to Jerusalem. Then they spot Him, sitting there in the Temple among the teachers; asking questions, listening to what they have to say. They were amazed at His knowledge and understanding. But Mary and Joseph were not amused. Then Jesus replies to them, "Why are you looking for me? Did you not know I had to be in my Father's house?"

He went back with them, in obedience, and in **Luke 2:52,** it says that Jesus grew in wisdom, and in stature. This is the first time that we see Jesus moving in the works of God. He's seeking His Father first. Hold on to that for a minute. Remember that. The first thing we see Jesus doing, is seeking God. We don't see Him, doing the rituals that had become so prevalent in that day. We see Him in the Temple, seeking God, going about His Father's business.[1]

In Mosaic law, it was considered work to spit on the ground. Therefore, you couldn't spit on the Sabbath. The reason for this is because it might turn up a tiny bit of dirt and that would be thought of as plowing the field. If you needed to spit, you had to go find a rock to do it on so as not to turn up that soil. The Pharisees must have thought about spitting a lot because they also thought about that spit mixing with the dirt. That would make it into mud, which would be thought of as mortar, thus breaking the Sabbath. Sounds to me like a bunch of men sitting around trying to one up each other in thinking of ways to not break one of God's laws. These guys took it to the extreme, God said to keep the day holy, to rest.

---

[1] Luke 2:41-52 NIV

These guys made it more work just to keep up with their ridiculous laws. Would it be more work to just spit where you were and make some mud, or walk five hundred feet looking for a rock? This is what God said about keeping the Sabbath:

Exodus 20:8-10, NIV

Remember the Sabbath day by keeping it holy. ⁹ Six days you shall labor and do all your work, ¹⁰ but the seventh day is a Sabbath to the LORD your God. On it you shall not do any work, neither you, nor your son or daughter, nor your male or female servant, nor your animals, nor any foreigner residing in your towns. ¹¹ For in six days the LORD made the heavens and the earth, the sea, and all that is in them, but he rested on the seventh day. Therefore the LORD blessed the Sabbath day and made it holy.

God commanded this because He knew we needed rest, not because He ever meant for us to keep ridiculous customs. Man took what God intended and perverted it to elevate themselves. It became a game of "who can be the holiest" when they were coming up with all of the ways that they would be breaking a command. All God wanted was for us to sit back from our hard labor of the week and enjoy Him. He wants us to bask in His presence.

Jesus broke these Jewish laws, a lot. This is one of the reasons that caused the Sadducees and the Pharisees to want Him dead. The reason Jesus broke these traditional laws was to prove to them, and us that they weren't what God required in the first place.

Picture Jesus walking down the road on the Sabbath with His disciples. They spot a blind man, blind from birth. And the disciples ask "Hey, Jesus. What did this man do wrong to be blind? Did he sin, or his parents?" Jesus tells them they are asking the wrong questions. It's not about what he did wrong, or what his parents might have done, but that the might of God will be displayed.[2] I want us to stop and really talk about this for a minute. There is no work that you can do, no sin that you can commit that can, or will, keep God from moving in your life. There are so many times, we think that the bad things that have happened to us are God's punishment on our lives. Instead, have you ever thought that He allows it so His Glory will be revealed to you in a deep and intimate way? If we understand who we are to Him, and who He truly is, there isn't anything that we face that His Glory won't shine in .

Back to the mud making that the Pharisees hate so much. Jesus could have just waved His hand over the

---

[2] John 9:1-5, NIV

blind man's eye. He could have spoken it to be healed, He could have done the Hokey Pokey and seen it healed. However, He chose to do it in a way that would stir up the religious people. He made mud! He made mud on the Sabbath! Oh, the blasphemy!

John 9:6-7, The Message

He said this and then spit in the dust, made a clay paste with the saliva, rubbed the paste on the blind man's eyes, and said, "Go, wash at the Pool of Siloam" (Siloam means "Sent"). The man went and washed—and saw.

Think about how scandalous this was. Here was this Rabbi, who claims to be the Messiah that everyone has been looking for going out of His way, not only to heal someone on the Sabbath, but to do so by spitting on the ground, making mud. In a way He was spitting on their traditions and man-made laws.

The town starts buzzing with the gossip. I would imagine it would be front page news that the blind from birth beggar man had gotten complete healing. Even bigger news that it was on the Sabbath. Even bigger news that the healer used his spit to make mud. They start questioning him, asking who was this man who healed him. They asked how it was done, and after they found out, they ran off to tell the Pharisees. They were divided, some were saying that Jesus couldn't have been from God because He violated the Sabbath. Others said that only a man of God could have done such an act. The blind man's parents were in fact, so afraid of the Jewish leaders at that time that they basically said "Go ask our son. He is of age." They were terrified that they would be thrown out of the synagogue because anyone that said Jesus was the Messiah was facing that fate. They start insulting the formally blind man, I imagine it was starting to become quite a circus. When questioned again about who healed him, the man again said it was Jesus. Then when the leaders started making comments about how they weren't even sure where Jesus was from, the man says this:[3]

John 9:30-33, NIV

30 The man answered, "Now that is remarkable! You don't know where he comes from, yet he opened my eyes. 31 We know that God does not listen to sinners. He listens to the godly person who does his will. 32 Nobody has ever heard of opening the eyes of a man born blind. 33 If this man were not from God, he could do nothing."

They then proceeded to throw the man out, saying he

---

[3] John 9 NIV

was a sinner from birth. Jesus goes to the man and asks him if he believes in the Son of Man. He exclaims. "Show him to me and I'll believe!" Jesus, tells him that he is looking at Him in the face, and the man believes. The next exchange between Jesus and the Pharisees, shows the stark difference between the true believer and the one who believes and gets their works mixed into true faith.

John 9:40-41

⁴⁰ Some Pharisees overheard him and said, "Does that mean you're calling us blind?" ⁴¹ Jesus said, "If you were really blind, you would be blameless, but since you claim to see everything so well, you're accountable for every fault and failure."

Jesus didn't come to uphold the traditions of man. We are steeped deep in traditions of religion. His acts really separate what was from God and what is man's own made up laws. It is so important for us to understand these things so we can tear down all of those strongholds that we have thought were correct for so long. This is one reason we have such a problem understanding who God truly is. Until we can see who our Father is, we have a hard time understanding who we truly are.

These leaders couldn't even see Jesus for who He was

and He was standing right in front of them. They were so blinded by their own driving desires to be right that they couldn't see God made flesh right in front of them, even when He was healing the blind.

Another tradition that Jesus blew out of the water was the washing of hands before they sat down to eat. I'm all for hand washing before you eat, but these guys were doing it to be make themselves feel more holy. There are the disciples sitting down to eat, they were starving after a long day of traveling and healing the sick. There were no spoons or forks then, so they would eat using their hands or a small piece of bread to scoop up foods that were more liquid. There was usually just one bowl or basket that was placed in the middle between everyone to share. So you can see that hand washing was probably a good idea. It just wasn't ever supposed to be part of the law. It's a prime example of us taking something that is good for us and making it God's decree when it never was to begin with.

Jesus addresses these Pharisees after they are confronted. His words are pretty harsh when it comes to what they have been doing.

Mark 7:6-8, The Message

6-8 Jesus answered, "Isaiah was right about frauds like you, hit the bull's-eye in fact:

These people make a big show of saying the right thing,
   but their heart isn't in it.
They act like they are worshiping me,
   but they don't mean it.
They just use me as a cover
   for teaching whatever suits their fancy,
Ditching God's command
   and taking up the latest fads."

He doesn't even stop there. He continues on telling them that they themselves are breaking God's Law.

Mark 7:9-13, The Message

9-13 He went on, "Well, good for you. You get rid of God's command so you won't be inconvenienced in following the religious fashions! Moses said, 'Respect your father and mother,' and, 'Anyone denouncing father or mother should be killed.' But you weasel out of that by saying that it's perfectly acceptable to say to father or mother, 'Gift! What I owed you I've given as a gift to God,' thus relieving yourselves of obligation to father or mother. You scratch out God's Word and scrawl a whim in its place. You do a lot of things like this."

Jesus pointed out that they have changed God's Law to make it more convenient for them. Don't we do this? I hear it all of the time. We justify our wrongdoing and say it is in the best interest of the church. We say we are defending the gospel. Changing God's Law's to fit our own wants and desires. We do it with His promises too, to fit our misconception that we don't deserve them, but more on that later.

The question has been raised. Should we eat as the Jewish people did? Is it okay for me to have that huge bundle of bacon on my cheeseburger? Other than the fact that it's not all that healthy to consume on a daily basis. Jesus says in the next few passages that all things are clean, that it's not what goes in our mouths that is of concern but what comes out of our mouths. We will also come back to why that is so important later.

Mark 7:18-19, The Message

18-19 Jesus said, "Are you being willfully stupid? Don't you see that what you swallow can't contaminate you? It doesn't enter your heart but your stomach, works its way through the intestines, and is finally flushed." (That took care of dietary quibbling; Jesus was saying that *all* foods are fit to eat.)

If we go back to the very first time that we see Jesus do something that would have been considered breaking the Sabbath, you see what I've been talking about. They were more concerned about this tradition being broken than following the Commandments that God Himself gave.

Back in Jesus day, the welfare system was that it was legal if you were passing by a field as you were traveling to break off a stalk of grain to eat it. You had to eat it while you were in the man's field, and you could not carry any away with you in a basket or wagon. You also were not allowed to harvest it with any tool. The farmers weren't permitted to harvest their whole field. They were required to leave the outer edges for the needy.[4]

So one day, which happened to be the Sabbath, Jesus and His disciples were walking through a grainfield. I'm starting to think that the Pharisees were like our modern day paparazzi, because they were there too. I imagine if they had cameras they would have taken pictures to sell to the highest bidder of Jesus' so called escapades.

The Pharisees were so crazy with their not working on the Sabbath that if you even plucked a grey hair from

---

[4] Deuteronomy 23:25

your head it was considered work. They didn't accuse the disciples of stealing grain from the farmer's field. They accused them of threshing and harvesting. Here is what is interesting about this exchange between Jesus and His accusers. He doesn't bring up the Jewish rituals, but rather He responds to them with scripture. He quotes **1 Samuel 21:1-6** to them. That particular verse refers to David eating consecrated bread from the Tabernacle. No one was supposed to eat of this bread except for the descendants of Aaron. [5] That wasn't a rule that the rabbis made up but an actual law given by God. So, why do you think that it was okay for David to eat this bread from the Tabernacle that was only to be consumed by the priests? Because David and his men were God's people, and the needs of God's people always come before a religious ritual, even when those rituals are set in place by God. That is the heart of our Lord. He is more concerned about meeting our needs than our rituals and right ways of doing things. Think of it like this, perhaps the rule at your house is that you always sit down to eat dinner as a family. That's a good family law, yet if your

---

[5] Leviticus 24:9

child came to you hungry before it was time to sit down, would you not meet their need? Of course you would. How much better of a Father do we have.

While Jesus was responding to the Pharisees accusations that they were harvesting on the Sabbath He says something that will wreck your way of thinking about all of the laws of the Sabbath.

Luke 6:5

[5] Then Jesus said to them, "The Son of Man is Lord of the Sabbath."

Jesus is the Lord of the Sabbath. He can do as He sees fit on that day. That should be pretty freeing for you as you grow in learning the attributes of Jesus. You'll find He is way more concerned about our well-being than our rituals and traditions.

There are several more instances of Jesus healing on the Sabbath. I won't go over each of them, but the thing we need to take away from this is that Jesus did break laws, laws that were set in place by religious leaders who were trying to elevate themselves to a place of being more holy that they really thought they were deep down inside.

So often we are guilty of doing things, reading our

Bible in the morning for instance, with a heart of doing it to gain favor with God. While the act of reading our Bible is a good thing, it is our heart that God is actually looking at. There is nothing we can do to gain more favor. There is nothing we can do to lose favor. You will always be God's favorite son or daughter.

Don't be in bondage to the law that Jesus came to set you free from. Don't put yourself into bondage with your own laws and rules. Do the things in Law because of your relationship with God, because you are a reflection of Him.

> Mirrors show us what we look like, not who we are.
>
> -Unknown

IDENTITY CRISIS

2 MIRROR, MIRROR

When you look in the mirror, what do you see? Do you see a person that looks unfamiliar staring back at you? Do you see someone you hate? Love? Do you see pieces of your mother and father? What do you see? Do you see that you are a reflection of God?

Just thinking about us being a mirror image of our Father just blows me out of the water. For so long I saw all of my shortcomings, the reasons I thought God couldn't love me. The mistakes from my past, the flaws in my body. The imperfections in my figure, the tiny details about my face that I didn't like. I wasn't able to see my reflection as it truly is. I was looking at a shell and not my Spirit man. Even more true than that, I wasn't looking at Jesus.

Personal story time. There were things about my past, things done to me that skewed the way I saw myself. The past became like a funhouse mirror distorting all that I saw in regards to my life.

When I was five years old, I was raped by a family member. This went on for years. The abuse was so bad that I have blocked out most of it. The things that remained were the words spoken over me and they shaped how I saw myself, both physically and spiritually. I was physical proof of **Proverbs 18:21**. I was dying inside from the lies about my identity. In return, I wanted to die physically. It left me questioning God. How could a loving Father leave a five year old to a monster like that? It shaped how I viewed men, most importantly, how I viewed Jesus. I felt unprotected, unloved, and dirty. When I looked in the mirror every morning, I didn't see an amazing girl with the heart of her Father's. I saw a broken, tired, used up wreck of a mess.

There were nights when I was between five and twelve, that I would sleep on the hardwood floor because I felt I was undeserving of a soft warm bed. I would look in a physical mirror and see a fat, unlovable, unwanted disaster. Most of my life, these were the things I saw. Everything was distorted beyond recognition of Truth.

What I didn't know, what I didn't see, was that I was the exact reflection of Jesus.

2 Corinthians 3:18 NIV

And we all, who with unveiled faces contemplate the Lord's glory, are being transformed into his image with ever-increasing glory, which comes from the Lord, who is the Spirit.

Transformed into His image. Ever-increasing glory. How good is that? Doesn't that just make you want to run off to a mirror and see the ever-increasing glory shining on your face?

If Jesus is the express image of God, and we are a reflection of Jesus, wouldn't you say we must be some of the most beautiful creatures on the earth? Why do we buy into the lies of the media, telling us we need to look like one very small percentage of the human population? Why don't we see the Glory of the Lord that has transformed us into His image?

Think about this, when we say that we aren't worth anything, when we look at disgust at ourselves, we are saying that God's creation isn't good. I'm an artist, and when I create something I want everyone to think it's good. I put everything I have into creating, and it hurts my heart when it's not received well, especially by those that I love. I believe that is the way God feels when we put ourselves down. All He sees in us is beauty, all He sees is Himself, which is pure Love.

Genesis 1:26-27 NIV

²⁶ Then God said, "Let us make mankind in our image, in our likeness, so that they may rule over the fish in the sea and the birds in the sky, over the livestock and all the wild animals,[a] and over all the creatures that move along the ground."

²⁷ So God created mankind in his own image, in the image of God he created them; male and female he created them.

How can we then, knowing that we were created in the very image of God, think we are not beautiful beyond our imagination? To say this, is to say that God is not beautiful, that He is not good, that He is unworthy.

We can't know what we truly look like until we know what the person we reflect looks like. I think this is a lot of the breakdown in how we see ourselves. We have forgotten to look at the right mirror image. We have forgotten to seek what Jesus looks like in order to see what we truly look like.

So let's look at the character of God so we know who we mirror. We know that God is love. I think most of society equates love with emotions and feelings. D.C. Talk says love is a verb. I have to disagree with all of those things. Love is God. Plain and simple. You cannot have Love without God. You cannot love someone else without Love, you cannot be loved without Love.

1 John 4:7-10 The Message

7-10 My beloved friends, let us continue to love each other since love comes from God. Everyone who loves is born of God and experiences a relationship with God. The person who refuses to love doesn't know the first thing about God, because God *is* love—so you can't know him if you don't love. This is how God showed his love for us: God sent his only Son into the world so we might live through him. This is the kind of love we are talking about—not that we once upon a time loved God, but that he loved us and sent his Son as a sacrifice to clear away our sins and the damage they've done to our relationship with God.

God is Love. If we don't understand anything else about God, about what we reflect to the world, understand that. We so often view God as anything but loving. Someone to punish us for getting it wrong, someone to only give us so many chances before He throws up His hands and walks way.

If God is Love. Then what is Love? We've all read **1 Corinthians**, but let's take a deeper look into that passage and really draw out what that means in our lives. What it means for us as we look at our Father, and also what it means for us as we look at ourselves.

1 Corinthians 13:4-13 NIV

⁴ Love is patient, love is kind. It does not envy, it does not boast, it is not proud. ⁵ It does not dishonor others, it is not self-seeking, it is not easily angered, it keeps no record of wrongs. ⁶ Love does not delight in evil but rejoices with the truth. ⁷ It always protects, always trusts, always hopes, always perseveres.
⁸ Love never fails. But where there are prophecies, they will cease; where there are tongues, they will be stilled; where there is knowledge, it will pass away. ⁹ For we know in part and we prophesy in part, ¹⁰ but when completeness comes, what is in part disappears. ¹¹ When I was a child, I talked like a child, I thought like a child, I reasoned like a child. When I became a man, I put the ways of childhood behind me. ¹² For now we see only a reflection as in a mirror; then we shall see face to face. Now I know in part; then I shall know fully, even as I am fully known.

¹³ **And now these three remain: faith, hope and love. But the greatest of these is love.**

Love is patient. God is patient. You are patient. That means when you screw up, fail, fall down, run from God so hard you don't think you will ever come back, God is patient with you. He doesn't get frustrated and start throwing lightning bolts down on your house. He lovingly and patiently waits for you.

You are patient. That means you are also patient with yourself. This is not a Kingdom of having patience for everyone else and not for yourself. You are patience. You embody it, it is your very essence just like your Father's.

Love is kind. God is kind. You are kind. God doesn't pull you up out of a miry pit only to turn around and push you back down in the mud. He not only picks you up, washes you off tenderly, but puts you on solid ground. He provides for your every need in a kind way. You are kindness. You have a sweet spirit about you in all that you do. It is who you are.

Love does not envy. God does not envy. You do not envy. There is the noun envy and the verb envy. The noun means a discontentment or longing regarding someone else's possessions, position, or power. The verb, of course, is that active desire. God already possesses all things. So naturally He doesn't envy. But, do you understand that you too, possess all that God has? He gave it to you already when you became one with Christ. So not only don't you envy, you have no need to do so, because all things are already yours.

Love does not boast. God does not boast. You do not boast. If anyone could boast and get away with it, it's God, but even He is humble. That one is hard for me to wrap my mind around, but it comes down to this, we are as He is. We need to be humble, so He is humble. We don't need to go around shouting about what we've done for the Kingdom. That in itself will be our reward. You do not boast. You only boast in what Jesus has done for you. [6]

Love is not proud. God is not proud. You are not proud. God doesn't get a swelled head about all the awesomeness that He has created. He doesn't go around being a narcissist about creating the universe and us and everything else in it. You, by the same token, don't get all bigheaded by thinking your accomplishments are what make you good. We aren't talking about healthy pride here. We should take pride in the way we look, or the way we present ourselves. We can be proud of our accomplishments without it becoming a fault. You are not proud or puffed up.

Love does not dishonor others. God does not dishonor

---

[6] Galatians 6:14

others. You do not dishonor others. God doesn't push Himself on others. He doesn't force His way into our hearts and lives. He waits for an invitation for us to realize He has been there all along and has never left us.

I've recently lost a friend that I would lay down my life for. I did nothing against this person, but they decided to leave anyway. I have wanted to barge back into their lives and force them to see the truth, but because I am a reflection of Jesus, I can't. I honor this person, by honoring their wishes, and I'm patient by waiting for them to realize the weight of Grace that I have seen. There is beauty in walking away. There is beauty in honor.

Love is not self-seeking. God is not self-seeking. You are not self-seeking. God doesn't go around with a me-first attitude. Otherwise, He never would have given us His son. Oh, the exquisiteness in that! To love us so much He laid down His own life, suffered all of humanity, just to bring us back into relationship to Himself. It just wrecks me every time I think about the measurement of that kind of love. I have to stop what I'm doing and praise Him in awe and wonder that He desired me that much.

You are not self-seeking. You are a God-seeker. You put others before yourself. You don't see it as a chore or something to mark off your list, you see it as pure joy to give to others before yourself. When you give, you do it with a heart of generosity, not self-seeking a reward for doing something for someone in gain.

Love is not easily angered. God is not easily angered. You are not easily angered. I know this is contrary to many of the things we believe about God. We believe that God is full of wrath. So many of us believe He gets angry at the slightest little thing we do wrong. This is simply untrue. God isn't mad at you. He has never been mad at you. It's not in His nature. I think the things He does get mad at, are when things hurt you. When He sees injustice happening to His beloved. But He is always fair and just toward His children. You are not easily angered. It is not in your nature to have road rage. It is not part of you to become enraged at your spouse or a friend. You don't fly off the handle at every little thing.

Love keeps no records of wrong. God keeps no records of wrong. You keep no records of wrong. God isn't sitting up there with a scoreboard jumbotron with your rights on one side and your wrongs on another. He doesn't even remember your wrongs. He has thrown them as far as the east is to the west. [7] He's not keeping them locked away in some hidden book only to pull them out and remind Himself of them later. He doesn't bring them up when you fall down again. He will never say to you, "Remember when you did that in college? You're

---

[7] Psalms 103:12

going to screw up your life forever because of that." If you hear that voice, know for certain it's not from God.

Because you are a mirror of God, you keep no records of wrongs. You don't make a list of everything people have done against you. You don't keep a mental running list of the things people have failed at. You don't even remember the wrongs. You are always looking toward the good.

Love does not rejoice in evil. God does not rejoice in evil. You do not rejoice in evil. God doesn't get His jollies by watching bad things happen to you. He doesn't like it when people are killed by natural disasters, or cancer, or accidents. Even the worst person we can imagine, God has love for. God doesn't rejoice in the evil they have done, but He does rejoice in the good in them. You don't rejoice when your neighbor you can't stand gets a new car and immediately wrecks it. You don't rejoice when someone that has hurt you so much you can't breathe, loses someone in the same way they hurt you. Your heart is so full of compassion that it aches even for those who have tried to destroy your life. You are your Father's reflection.

Love rejoices in truth. God rejoices in truth. You rejoice in truth. Think of this, Jesus said He was the Way, the Truth and the Life. [8] We rejoice in Jesus. God

---

[8] John 14:6

rejoices every single time we recognize a lie against ourselves, against Him. God rejoices in everything that is true.

Love always protects. God always protects. You always protect. I know sometimes we don't feel that we are protected. When our world is falling apart, when we feel vulnerable, we often wonder where God is. Our finances don't feel protected, our relationships are on the edge, our lives are in danger, but the truth is, we are completely safe and protected in God's arms.

There is one particular person in my life that I feel could take on the world for me. I have never felt so safe as when this person is walking beside me. He is big and strong, and I know he would lay down his very life to protect mine. He could squash someone with one hand if need be.

Most of my life I haven't felt safe. I have had many things happen to me over the course of my life that have made me feel very vulnerable to the world. I have come to realize, as safe as my friend makes me feel, Jesus is an even better bodyguard. He has legions and legions of angels right at the sound of His voice to come and rescue us. He doesn't even want us to dash our foot against a stone.[9] He is Kevin Costner to our Whitney Houston, only a trillion times more.

---

[9] Psalms 91:12

Love always trusts. God always trusts. You always trusts. I admit I exhibit trust issues. For so long I struggled to trust God, but God is the only one I have found that is completely worthy of my trust.

Love always hopes. God always hopes. You always hope. God is always looking for the positive. He is always looking for the good. You always look for the good in people. You always wait with expectancy that good is happening.

Love perseveres. God perseveres. You preserver. God doesn't give up on you. Ever. God doesn't work on coming into relationship with you for a while and then give up when the going gets tough. God doesn't love you for a while and then decide it's too complicated. Like we discussed in chapter one, He has had this planned out since before the foundation of the earth. That, my friend is perseverance. You don't give up when the going gets tough. You are in this for the long haul. You love fiercely and without condition, after all, you are a reflection of God.

Love never fails. God never fails. You never fail. God doesn't fail us. We don't fail God. Take that and put it deep, deep, deep in your heart. Let it grow there as a tiny seed, planting roots, growing tall limbs. Let it permeate your very being.

There is nothing that you can do to make God look at you with anything but complete love. He IS love.

Whenever the thoughts come to you that you're not worthy of Him, know that He cannot look at you in any other way but with pure love. Every single aspect of love that we see in **1 Corinthians 13** applies to how God sees you one hundred percent of the time.

Whoo-hoo-hoo, look who knows so much. It just so happens that your friend here is only MOSTLY dead. There's a big difference between mostly dead and all dead. Mostly dead is slightly alive. With all dead, well, with all dead there's usually only one thing you can do.

-Miracle Max, The Princess Bride

3 DIE ALREADY

Let the funeral procession begin. Cue the requiem. Listen to the drumbeat. This one is hard for me, but the truth is, we were slain with Christ before the foundation of the world.

Revelation 13:8, NIV

All inhabitants of the earth will worship the beast—all whose names have not been written in the Lamb's book of life, the Lamb who was slain from the creation of the world.

Galatians 2:20, NIV

I have been crucified with Christ and I no longer live, but Christ lives in me. The life I now live in the body, I live by faith in the Son of God, who loved me and gave himself for me.

I know understanding this is really hard for some of us. We want to live in the flesh so bad because It's all we've ever known. Living in the realm of God, as He sees us, is an uncommon event for even the most hardcore Christian. The truth is though, we already live there. We are already dead.

The first time I thought about that, or admitted to myself that I was dead, it made panic rise up in me. Death is so final. I've lost so many of my loved ones to death that it is the last thing I want to think about, much less experience. What if I want that old comfortable nature back? If it's dead I can't get it back, and so the cycle of fear and then resolve began. There is no such thing as "mostly dead" outside of fairytales, so I have to choose. Death to come alive or being alive to come to death.

There is no striving in the death. We don't try to become dead to sin. We don't try to die to our desires and wants. Dead people can't do anything except, well, be dead. I have so often fought and fought to die to the things that I want. Desires that well up inside of me that are truly from God, but because of past pain I try to dismiss them and say I don't deserve these beautiful things.

I push so much of what God wants for me in my life away, just simply because of fear. I think to myself, *"Oh, I can't have that. That's too big for God."* Or *"I don't deserve that, Papa. Give that to someone else."* We think that we are dying to self when we do this. Dying to our desires. What if those desires we are dying to, were the whispers of our Father to our hearts? What if He is the one that put that deep inside of you and every time you try to die to it, He is unable to make the good things come alive?

Psalms 37:4 NIV

Take delight in the LORD,
and he will give you the desires of your heart.

Notice it doesn't say, wish real hard for something and God will give you the desires of your heart. It doesn't say, if you are good, and worthy and read your Bible every day that God will give you the desires of your heart. It doesn't say, die and kill all of the desires in your heart so that you can please Papa. The only thing He has called us to do for our desires, is to take delight in the Lord.

Philippians 1:6 NIV

being confident of this, that he who began a good work in you will carry it on to completion until the day of Christ Jesus.

Don't you think that the God who is good enough to put the desire in your heart in the first place, is good enough to carry it out and complete the good work in you?

So what does it mean to delight yourself in the Lord? It simply means to take great pleasure in the Lord. When you finally understand the depth and breadth of His love for you, delighting in Him, delighting in that Love, comes pretty easy.

When He says He will give you the desires of your heart, does this mean that He will grant every single whim of your mind? I don't believe this is it at all. I believe when we start delighting ourselves in Him, in His great love for us, our desires and His desires align into one single road. He is faithful to not only put those desires in your heart, but also to fulfill them, as He promised in **Philippians 1:6**.

So we have no need, as long as we are resting, and

delighting in the Lord, to try to kill off the desires in our hearts. They are blessed and put there by Jesus Himself. I know sometimes those desires can be scary. They can be contrary to anything that you've ever wanted before. They can look impossible.

I really didn't like children much. The more I came into knowledge of Who I am, the more the desire to be around kids came into my heart. It started by holding a little four month old baby girl. I wouldn't even say it was a "she". I would say, *"Let me hold it."* Then about five minutes into it, I would shudder and hand her over to whoever would take her. I usually didn't have to go too far to find someone waiting to take my place.

Eventually I started calling her by her name, Addy. Then I got brave and changed a few diapers. Wet ones only, until one day, I wanted to hold her, rock her to sleep. There was something about the way she looked so peaceful and innocent that I fell in love with.

My dislike of children came out of pain. There was a time in my life that I wanted nothing less than twenty-four kids. I was young and didn't understand the logistics of such a task, but still, it was my heart's desire to become a mother of many. As time passed, and I had miscarriage after miscarriage, my heart grew cold. Stone like. I was unable to see the joy in children at all, their constant neediness turned me off.

I was a former nanny, a former assistant manager to a

daycare. Gradually because of pain, I let the emptiness become my truth and I died to the desire that Papa put in me as a child. Even now, as I sit here writing this section of the book, my heart is overcome with grief at the loss.

The more I came to know Papa intimately the more He spoke to my heart on the subject. *"You know you really love kids."* He would whisper. I would deny it and dig in deeper to my dislike of their running and jumping and screaming with delight. How dare they have energy!

But the desire never went away. I would cry myself to sleep at night with the longing in my heart stinging and burning relentlessly. You see, when God places a desire in your heart, no circumstance can kill it. No amount of pain can dismiss it. He is faithful and just to complete it.

A few weeks ago, I texted my friend. *"What is happening to me? I suddenly like children."* His response back was one word. *"Jesus."* It kept building in me, the love of these children. I finally blurted it out in Women's Bible Study. *"God made me like kids."* One of the ladies started clapping joyfully, she said she knew Jesus would get me.

I am not sitting here with my daughter in my arms. I have not seen God fulfill His promise to me that He will send her. But, the more I find my delight in Him, the more the things I wanted to die come alive in me. I can't kill it off no matter what I do, because I was not the author of it. Nor am I the finisher of it. So I wait for

Him to fulfill His promise to bring me the desires of my heart in His good time.

What about our sin? We try so hard to kill off our sin inside of us. How can we kill off something that is already dead? We strive and push to eradicate our lives of the things that we feel guilty about. I am not saying that we should go out and sin. Exactly the opposite actually. Once we see that we are already dead to sin, we no longer live out of our sin nature.

We begin operating out of Love. A dead man can't steal, can't lie, can't watch porn at 3 a.m. A dead man can't do anything. This is probably going to be lost on some of you, but how many of you have seen *Weekend at Bernie's*? It's an old dark comedy about two guys who pretend their murdered boss is still alive. They put Bernie in all sorts of crazy situations, while the hit man that was sent to kill him, tries to finish off the job. How is that like our spiritual lives?

I think about this a lot, I'm just this dead man walking around with Jesus being the life in me. The enemy is still trying to take out someone who is already dead. The enemy can't kill or destroy something that is already dead, just like the hit man couldn't kill Bernie a second time.

Back to **Galatians 2:20**. I no longer live, but Christ lives in me. So, let me pose you with this question that will burn your sacred cow of religion to the ground. Can

Jesus sin?

Of course not. The Bible clearly says that Jesus was without sin. Blameless, the perfect lamb.

2 Corinthians 5:21 NIV

God made him who had no sin to be sin for us, so that in him we might become the righteousness of God.

1 John 3:5 NIV

You know that He appeared in order to take away sins; and in Him there is no sin.

So, if Jesus has no sin, and according to **Galatians 2:20,** we are dead and Jesus lives in us, then do we have a sin nature anymore?

Good news folks! Our sin nature is dead. We only sin out of not understanding who we are, or by willful choice. I can choose to sin, but it is not in my new nature to do so. I am pure Love, just like we talked about in chapter two.

This is super frightening to a lot of people because it takes it out of our hands, and most of us, like me, are control freaks. We want to say we tried hard and overcame the sin our lives. We want to get the credit for being a good little boy or girl. When in reality, you didn't do anything but die with Jesus on the cross. You didn't feel the pain. He did. You didn't take the lashes on your back. He did. You didn't have a crown of thorns embedded into your brow. He did. You got all of the benefit of the redemption without any of the pain. You died on that cross with Him, and felt none of the agony. That, my friends, is a loving Father.

When you find yourself slipping back into things of the old self, stop and ask yourself, *"Does a redeemed person do this?"* If it doesn't line up to who you are in Christ, then it's not for you. We so often buy into the lie that we can't help but to sin. It has been so engrained in us that we are rotten dirty sinners that when we do fall back into the old ways, we justify it. We need to renew our minds in those moments and remember that the old is dead and the new has come.

Romans 6:11 NIV

In the same way, count yourselves dead to sin but alive to God in Christ Jesus.

So, we've talked about being dead. Let's look at the flip side of that and look at being alive. What exactly does being alive to God in Christ Jesus look like?

I will say this- it isn't always an easy journey. When

we start to walk in the footsteps that Jesus took, we are faced with many things that He faced Himself. Persecution. Physical suffering. Death.

Matthew 13:57 NIV

And they took offense at him. But Jesus said to them, " A prophet is not without honor except in his own town and in his own home."

When you are living out the radical life of someone who is walking in the authority of knowing who they are in Christ, you will be persecuted for it. The people that you grew up with will suddenly not understand you. Your family might turn their backs, refusing to listen to the new Truths that you have learned. People don't like to be wrong. They like to be comfortable.

You can be full of joy, and full of life at the same time you are being left by the wayside. I have found that God has cut out many of the people from my past, and I'm not just talking about those people that you would think He would remove. There's beauty in the refinement though.

When you understand that you don't belong in this world, that God made you and purposed you for so much more, the hurtful things people say seem to roll off your back. There comes a point where you feel compassion for their lack of knowledge instead of being hurt by their words and actions.

Jesus wasn't accepted in His own hometown, and because He is living inside of us, we can expect the same. I have found those that are Christians without the understanding of grace are the ones that are most offended, much like the Pharisees we talked about in chapter one. They did not like or understand what Jesus was saying or doing. They wanted Him dead for it.

When we are alive in Christ, the things of this world seem to fade away. I'm not saying we don't enjoy baseball games or a good movie, but our priority shifts so drastically that we just naturally live out of a different place than the rest of the world does. When we go to that baseball game, we are no longer going just to root on our favorite team, but we are looking at it as walking in Glory wherever we go.

Suddenly the sunset over the stadium becomes brighter, the colors come alive with the pinks and oranges. We recognize our Father's handiwork in everything. The umpire that just made a questionable call, isn't just some jerk guy out to ruin your good time, but a human that God created and loved and formed in His own image.

When we become alive in Christ our whole perspective changes. We see beauty in everything. We see Love in every human being. We see our Father in every single aspect of existence.

With beauty, comes pain. God makes beauty from ashes.[10] For there to be ashes, something has to be burned. I think of the funeral pyre. Wood piled high, set ablaze burning the dead into ashes. Refinement of sorts. We are being refined day by day, minute by minute. As our relationship with Jesus becomes more intimate, the more dross is removed.

While I was in prayer a few weeks ago, Papa showed me that I am like a diamond. Most of my life, I have been hard pressed. Compressed. Unthinkable things have happened to me. I have endured much pain, both physically and emotionally.

A diamond is formed from carbon that has endured crushing pressure and intense heat. That tension is what makes the diamond the hardest substance on earth. It makes it impossibly strong. The beauty is formed violently, much like my own beauty was formed out of violence and force. Without the duress, the inside of me wouldn't have been made strong. It would have lacked beauty.

Diamonds can be used as tools. They can cut with precision on even very hard surfaces. They make excellent engraving tools for this very reason. The strongest substance is what can engrave on the stone

---

[10] Isaiah 61:3

hearts of men.

2 Corinthians 3:3 NIV

You show that you are a letter from Christ, the result of our ministry, written not with ink but with the Spirit of the living God, not on tablets of stone but on tablets of human hearts.

He keeps expanding my understanding of this. How a diamond in the rough isn't much to look at. If you don't know what you're looking for, you will miss it all together as something precious.

In Arkansas, not far from where I grew up, there is an actual diamond mine. It's called the Crater of Diamonds State Park, in Murfreesboro.[11] I remember going there as a small child with my parents and a couple of neighbors. What I remember the most was the dry black dirt and the heat of the day. I didn't know what I was looking for, but I was happy to play in the dirt for once without getting in trouble. It was hard work looking for this tiny speck of something shiny among all of the other rocks and dirt. No one in our group found a diamond that day.

Even when the dirt is washed away from the diamond

---

[11] www.craterofdiamondsstatepark.com

it's still dull, it has no luster and doesn't reflect the light. What Papa has shown me lately is that it takes a Master cutter, a Master craftsman to cut away the inclusions, to shine it up, to know the best way for it to reflect the light. A particular cut for that particular diamond. You can't just cut a diamond into any shape you want. It takes a trained eye to see what should be cut away and what should be kept.

Wars are fought and blood is shed over diamonds. In the Congo and in Sierra Leone, civil wars are financed by blood diamonds. Bloodshed is always part of a sacrifice. As Papa showed me the truth of being a diamond, He also revealed to me in a deeper way the Blood that was shed for me.

The closer I come in relationship with God, the more inclusions are naturally cut away by the Master Cutter. The more I reflect His Light, His image. It's not that I've become anything that I wasn't already. I was always a stunning diamond underneath, but as I become alive in Christ, the beauty of the reflection is revealed.

Have you ever watched a diamond reflect from a stage? When a spotlight hits a real diamond in just the right way, it can become blinding. Imagine how bright God's light can be reflected when we start to come alive to Him. When the roughness and the false identity starts to be cut away to reveal what we've been all along. Our lives start to live out beauty for ashes. The cutting away isn't quite as painful. With each new step of the process of shedding my old mindsets, more brilliance is revealed.

The people that have given their lives for living out of the Kingdom amaze me. I wonder sometimes if I would have the strength to do that. To go where it's uncomfortable, to lay down my life for my friends.[12] The truth is, when you know who you are, fear fades. I no longer am afraid to die at the hands of a stranger. I spent a lot of my life fearing that very thing. Fearing death at the hands of someone I know is even worse.

I had a conversation with a childhood friend a couple of weeks ago that I won't soon forget. He has gone into ministry as well, working with the homeless. My passion is for women and the homeless, so the work that he does is close to my heart. I was talking with him about facing something that was very difficult for me, and it came up that I would be doing this alone. He said he feared for my safety. It touched my heart so deeply, because he understands what it is like to go minister to those people that society has forgotten. I had to say though, that though my heart was grieved greatly, I was not afraid. There is no persecution that I can face that will in anyway come close to equaling what my Jesus suffered on the cross just so that God would no longer be an enemy in my own mind.[13] Resting in that peace, knowing that no

---

[12] John 15:13

[13] Colossians 1:21

matter what the suffering, we are one with our Father. That is becoming alive in Christ.

Acts 20:24 NIV

I consider my life worth nothing to me, if only I may finish the race and complete the task the Lord Jesus has given me, the task of testifying to the gospel of God's grace.

The task at hand is to testify to the gospel of God's grace. Everything else fades away into the background like music at a shopping mall. You're aware that it's there, but no one is really paying attention. The focus becomes shouting from the rooftops that you are dead and that Christ now is alive in you.

I'm a slave for you. I cannot hold it; I cannot control it.
				-Britney Spears

4

LOVE SLAVE

A lot of us have a slave mentality. Just like the Israelites wandering around in the desert for forty long hot years. They had been slaves so long that they couldn't see themselves as free. The ones that were set free had been born into slavery, so they had no concept of what freedom really was.

Slavery wasn't fun, but at least they knew what was expected. How difficult it must have been to suddenly not know what the rules were. With slavery came their food and housing, their security. Stepping out into freedom, they had to rely on God completely to supply those needs that were never an issue before. Would the manna be there tomorrow morning? Would their shoes and clothes wear out even though He promised they wouldn't? Where would water come from? A rock? The Israelites were so bound up in fear and complaining that they couldn't accurately see all of the provisions and blessings that God had put before them. Sure, now they didn't have someone breathing down their back telling them every move to make, but there was a sense of being comfortable in that very thing.

How do you learn to dance when you've never seen someone take a twirl to the music? Freedom was so foreign a concept to them that they didn't know what foot to put in front of the other. They looked to Moses for what to do, but found themselves complaining and falling right back into old patterns.

After the American Civil War, many of the slaves decided to remain where they were. They had food and housing, clothing and a job. It was all that they had known, and stepping out into the big bad world without that comfort, without the shackles, seemed daunting. Fear of the unknown, became the chains. Lack of confidence became the whip against their backs.

Stockholm syndrome. Are we so used to our former life as a slave that we actually identify with the enemy camp? Do we identify with our aggressor, believing the same values so that they cease to become a threat?[i] Have we become so used to the lies we tell ourselves that we can't be anything but slaves to our own desires, our own sins?

The Israelites that came out of the slavery weren't allowed to enter into the Promised Land, not because of their sin, but because of their mindset. They never left the slavery behind. They never understood that they could walk in the fullness of the Kingdom that Papa had set before them.

I experienced this in my former abusive marriage. Coming out of that, I had such a slave mentality. I didn't know what it was like to think for myself. I remember being in the middle of it, so unhappy, yet so afraid of losing my security. Security that was all an illusion in the first place. There is no safety outside of God.

I didn't know what it was like to not sleep with one eye open for five years straight. I never knew when I would say the wrong thing, and he would explode into a rage of curse words and demeaning insults. I believed the lie that it was my fault, that I upset him with my behavior. I thought, well, it's bad now, but it will be worse if I leave. So I stayed, way past time for me to get out for safety.

When I finally did leave, the slave mentality came with me for quite some time. It wasn't until I realized that Jesus set the captives free in a real way, not just with lip service was I able to break free of the chains tied around my heart to all of the misspoken words that were spewed in my direction.

Women stay, and often die, in these abusive relationships because they have no hope for their future. They can't see that there is any way to be taken care of, nurtured or loved again, even by our Good Papa. Even false love seems better than no love at all. Trusting someone to love them for real seems impossible, a fantasy. This kind of love becomes a false identity. We equate love with doing everything right. If I cook dinner just right, maybe he will love me. If I lose fifty pounds, maybe he will kiss me again like he used to. If I just keep silent, then maybe he won't push me up against the wall by my throat and tell me if I don't shut my mouth, he will shut it for me.

This kind of abuse carries over into how we view God, ourselves. If we are living in fear that we will anger Papa, we aren't able to live in the fullness of who He is. We become slaves to pleasing a Father who is already pleased with us, just so He won't abandon us. But the Bible says He will never leave us or forsake us.

Deuteronomy 31:8 NIV

It is the Lord who goes before you. He will be with you; he will not leave you or forsake you. Do not fear or be dismayed.

The thing about living under Grace, is I don't have ill will toward the people that have hurt me. I have released them from the prison of hate and I can pray for God to bless them with honesty and a pure heart.

We sometimes come out of religion with a slave mentality. We are taught in Sunday school to conform to the norm. We are told what to wear, Sunday best for Sunday morning. Signs of individuality are looked down upon. No tattoos, purple hair, or piercings if you want to make a difference in the Kingdom. Read this book, go to this conference, sign up for this marriage seminar if you want to your husband to still look at you with love when you've gained that baby weight and your boobs start to sag. Strive, strive, harder, faster, pray more, fast more, listen to this teacher, don't listen to that teacher. Join the choir and God will love you even more, God didn't give you the gift of your voice for you to waste it worshipping Him in the back row pew.

When did we stop having relationship with Papa? When did we stop looking into the eyes of our Savior with a burning passion to know Him more? When did we stop dancing with Holy Spirit? When did we become slaves in our own Sanctuary?

We can become a slave to our own thinking. So many people are held in bondage because the things of God aren't logical. I think this is in one way what the

Bible is talking about when it says we have made God our enemy in our own minds. [14]

People feel that if they can't figure God out then He can't be real. If God can't be based on science then He can't be true. Personally, I don't see how life evolving from one single cell organism to all of the species we have now makes more sense than a supreme and awesome eternal being creating us out of Love.

We have forgotten faith, and we only believe what we can see, feel, and touch. That doesn't work well in the Kingdom of God. He is a God of unexpected wonder. He is a God of mystery and romance. He is the one that created science and math and art and music to begin with. Yet so many people think that science lives outside the realm of God. *"I believe in Science."* They say with their heads held high. So do I. God created it.

It is such a lie to think we can only believe in what can be proven in this world. We are slaves to our own intellect, refusing to open our minds past what is concrete and what we think is factual.

One thing I've learned is with a slave mentality it's impossible to enter into your Promised Land. It's not that God doesn't want to grant you the things that He has spoken into your heart. He desperately is trying to get you to look Him straight in the eye and see His burning

---

[14] Colossians 1:21

passion and love for you.

You've probably asked yourself, like I have, why didn't God allow the Israelites that were set free to enter into the land He promised? We can act in two ways when we are hit with adversity. With the slave mentality, that we will never have anything good now, that being in the bondage was actually the better time, or we can choose to act with a mind of freedom. All things are ours when we choose freedom.

The Israelites complained about the manna. They wanted meat, and cucumbers and melons like they had when they were in Egypt. If they had shed their slave mindset and realized that they were free, they would have bolted into the Promised Land and had all of the milk and honey they could have taken in .

When we murmur, we are showing distrust in God to provide. I am guilty of this. I get so afraid that my needs will not be provided for, that I stay up all night worried. Even when I do sleep, I find myself waking up in a cold sweat worried about how I'm going to get things taken care of. This isn't how God wants me to react. He wants me to expectantly look with joy as to the ways He will provide. This slave mindset that I have grown accustomed to, the striving and working to earn my provision, is what is keeping God from being able to completely release His blessings into my life. I can't serve both masters. Either I am a slave to worry and struggle or I am free to reign as the adopted daughter of the King.

Just like the Israelites we forget to look back over what God has done, how He has provided in the past and look forward to the ways He will provide in the next situation. They didn't look back at the ways that He removed them from Pharaoh's rule. They didn't think back to when the Red Sea parted and they made their way safely to the other side. They didn't look fondly on manna falling from the sky to provide their daily bread. Instead, they fell back into the old ways. They worshipped a golden calf when they became insecure about Moses being up a mountain for forty days. [15]

Isaiah 61:1-3 NIV

The Spirit of the Sovereign LORD is on me,
  because the LORD has anointed me
  to proclaim good news to the poor.
He has sent me to bind up the brokenhearted,
  to proclaim freedom for the captives
  and release from darkness for the prisoners,
² **to proclaim the year of the LORD's favor**
  and the day of vengeance of our God,
to comfort all who mourn,
³   **and provide for those who grieve in Zion—**

---

[15] Ex 32:1-35

to bestow on them a crown of beauty
   instead of ashes,
the oil of joy
   instead of mourning,
and a garment of praise
   instead of a spirit of despair.
They will be called oaks of righteousness,
   a planting of the LORD
   for the display of his splendor.

Luke 4:16-20 NIV

[16] He went to Nazareth, where he had been brought up, and on the Sabbath day he went into the synagogue, as was his custom. He stood up to read, [17] and the scroll of the prophet Isaiah was handed to him. Unrolling it, he found the place where it is written:

[18] "The Spirit of the Lord is on me,
   because he has anointed me
   to proclaim good news to the poor.
He has sent me to proclaim freedom for the prisoners
   and recovery of sight for the blind,
to set the oppressed free,
[19]   to proclaim the year of the Lord's favor."[

20 Then he rolled up the scroll, gave it back to the attendant and sat down. The eyes of everyone in the synagogue were fastened on him. **21** He began by saying to them, "Today this scripture is fulfilled in your hearing."

Jesus came to set you free. It was prophesied in Isaiah and fulfilled on the cross. You are no longer a slave. The shackles you think are there, are self-imposed. The murmurs and complaints are without cause, you are free. You have all things that the Father has. You are free indeed.

John 8:34-38 The Message

34-38 Jesus said, "I tell you most solemnly that anyone who chooses a life of sin is trapped in a dead-end life and is, in fact, a slave. A slave is a transient, who can't come and go at will. The Son, though, has an established position, the run of the house. So if the Son sets you free, you are free through and through. I know you are Abraham's descendants. But I also know that you are trying to kill me because my message hasn't yet penetrated your thick skulls. I'm talking about things I have seen while keeping company with the Father, and you just go on doing what you have heard from your

father."

Embrace your freedom. Throw off the old mindset of slavery. Start living in the Castle instead of the slave's quarters. Sleep in a cushy king sized bed with velvet coverings instead of on a sack of straw. Eat a feast at the table, instead of the scraps from the kitchen. You are free.

The only kind of slave that we are is a Love Slave. When a slave is set free, yet chooses to stay with their master because of love, they are considered a bondservant. They've moved past the need to serve out of obligation or ownership, and have moved into something new, something different. They become a friend, a lover, anything but a slave.

When we chose to serve God out of relationship a beautiful thing happens. Jesus serves us, like He did the Disciples.[16] We in return, give our lives to serve Him because of our love. It's mutual. Not one owning or possessing the other.

If we turn our back on Him, He doesn't punish us, whip us, beat us into submission. He gently washes our feet, anoints our heads with oil. He dresses us in fine linen embroidered with pure gold thread. He puts rubies and sapphires around our necks. He adorns our noses

---

[16] John 13:1-20

with a ring of gold studded with diamonds. No matter how many times we turn to walk away, He is always there waiting to welcome us back into our rightful home as a son or daughter.

Realizing what that truly means, this sonship, leads us to want to dive deeper into relationship with Him. Where the Grace flows in and around us like an ocean. We sink to the bottom completely engulfed in His Love. In that Love, we find that we would gladly lay down our lives, give up any comfort just so we can serve Him out of our devotion and not fear. Fear of punishment has no place in this Father-child relationship. Even His wrath is burning with passionate Love.

I'm struggling with this right now. I've had to stop writing several times to realign my heart with the Truth. I believe that a teacher, writer, is only really effective when they tell the whole truth of the matter. I've been facing something impossibly hard the last few months. A place where the world, including well-meaning fellow believers are speaking into my life in a way that feels outside of who I know God to be. It makes me panic. It makes me struggle to find a solution on my own, rather than to rest in God's love for me. To please them, to "do the right thing" or "do what I'm supposed to be doing"

Over and over I quote to myself, *"Be anxious for nothing, but everything with prayer and supplication, with thanksgiving, make your requests known to God."*[17]

I'm free. Why do I let fear of lack of provision come in and invade my life? I'm completely and earnestly devoted to Jesus and my life with Him. Why do I suddenly turn back and have the mindset of the Israelites? Why do I fall back into the slave mentality that Jesus died to set me free from?

Because sometimes we forget that we are in relationship, not out of obligation, but based in His great Love for us. We forget that He promised to take care of our every need, not because we serve Him, but because He is good.

Being a Love Slave in the palace, means all I have to do is sit back and enjoy the riches of the King. A Love Slave is there for pleasure, to be lavished upon. We need to learn to rest in that role.

Let's take a look at the prodigal son. I know we all know the story backwards and forwards, but let's take a deeper look at it.

Luke 15:11-32 The Message

11-12 Then he said, "There was once a man who had two sons. The younger said to his father, 'Father, I want right now what's coming to me.'

---

[17] Philippians 4:6

¹²⁻¹⁶ "So the father divided the property between them. It wasn't long before the younger son packed his bags and left for a distant country. There, undisciplined and dissipated, he wasted everything he had. After he had gone through all his money, there was a bad famine all through that country and he began to hurt. He signed on with a citizen there who assigned him to his fields to slop the pigs. He was so hungry he would have eaten the corncobs in the pig slop, but no one would give him any.

¹⁷⁻²⁰ "That brought him to his senses. He said, 'All those farmhands working for my father sit down to three meals a day, and here I am starving to death. I'm going back to my father. I'll say to him, Father, I've sinned against God, I've sinned before you; I don't deserve to be called your son. Take me on as a hired hand.' He got right up and went home to his father.

²⁰⁻²¹ "When he was still a long way off, his father saw him. His heart pounding, he ran out, embraced him, and kissed him. The son started his speech: 'Father, I've sinned against God, I've sinned before you; I don't deserve to be called your son ever again.'

²²⁻²⁴ "But the father wasn't listening. He was calling to the servants, 'Quick. Bring a clean set of clothes and

dress him. Put the family ring on his finger and sandals on his feet. Then get a grain-fed heifer and roast it. We're going to feast! We're going to have a wonderful time! My son is here—given up for dead and now alive! Given up for lost and now found!' And they began to have a wonderful time.

25-27 "All this time his older son was out in the field. When the day's work was done he came in. As he approached the house, he heard the music and dancing. Calling over one of the houseboys, he asked what was going on. He told him, 'Your brother came home. Your father has ordered a feast—barbecued beef!—because he has him home safe and sound.'

28-30 "The older brother stalked off in an angry sulk and refused to join in. His father came out and tried to talk to him, but he wouldn't listen. The son said, 'Look how many years I've stayed here serving you, never giving you one moment of grief, but have you ever thrown a party for me and my friends? Then this son of yours who has thrown away your money on whores shows up and you go all out with a feast!'

31-32 "His father said, 'Son, you don't understand. You're with me all the time, and everything that is mine is yours—but this is a wonderful time, and we had

to celebrate. This brother of yours was dead, and he's alive! He was lost, and he's found!'"

It is impossible for me to not include the whole scripture verses when talking about the Prodigal Son. In truth though, the story really isn't about the lost son, it's about the Good Father.

We all pack up our bags and move to a distant land at some point in our walk with Papa. Maybe we build a wall because someone in the church hurt us. Maybe we rebel and go directly against what God asked of us like Jonah. Maybe we just aren't living in the knowledge of His great love for us and it causes us to turn away from Him out of fear. Whatever the foreign land looks like, we have all been there at some point.

We have all gotten to the bottom of the pig pen too. Think about this story for a minute. Why do you think that Jesus used a pig pen as part of the parable?

I have friends that are starting to become homesteaders. The last time I was in Arkansas, I stopped by their house to see them. As I was driving up the dirt driveway I looked to my right and saw a huge pig pen. I also saw a herd of tiny little mud covered pigs running. I stopped the car to look at them. I had never seen that many pigs in one place before, and I certainly had never seen them in their real environment. My only pig experiences come from Charlotte's Web, a big pink pig that tried to come in my house once when I was living in the country, and pigs that were clean being judged at the State Fair of Texas. I may be from Arkansas, but I am a city girl at heart.

I sat there in delight to watch these tiny piglets run across the mud. I was shocked as to how many of them that there were. Then I noticed stirring in the mud. There was a giant pig buried up to her snout in mud. She slowly rose to her feet and trotted off following the babies.

Then I understood something. When we first arrive at the pig pen, we are able to walk across the mud with ease. We don't sink deep into the mud with only our noses poking out so we can breathe in a little air. This pig was content. She was happy to be completely covered up in that cool mud. When she rose, she was slow and caked in filth.

For the Jewish people, for someone to go live with the pigs was one of the most disgraceful things one could think of. Pigs were considered the filthiest of the filthy. From that day looking into that pig pen, I'll agree for sure. This poor son, couldn't even get someone to give him the corn cobs.

Pay attention to this point. He goes back to the Father's house with a slavery mindset. He is thinking, if his Father will just let him work in the slave's quarters.

He was so desperate to be fed (how desperate do we get to be fed spiritually?) that he was willing to humble himself before his Dad and say that he was willing to become one of the servants.

What does the Father do though? He isn't sitting back on the front porch in disgust. If you've been living among the pigs, you are sure to smell like one. I can just see the son now, limping his way up the road, exhausted, covered in filth from head to toe. Mud caked in his hair. Pig dung and the remainder of slop dried onto his torn clothes. There wasn't anywhere for him to clean himself up along the way. He had to come there just as he was. The Father sees him coming toward the Palace and He races out to meet the son where he was. The Father throws His arms around him and kisses him. The Father gets dirty too.

That is how much we are loved. Jesus got dirty on our behalf. The Father doesn't even listen to the son's apology. He is already calling the servants to go and prepare a party. He's calling for clean clothes, and a family ring. The family ring is significant in our adoption into the family of God.

Take note of this. The elder son, the one who didn't go off to the pig pen, the one who did everything right, is also in bondage. He could have had the party the whole time as well, but instead he was a slave to doing "everything right".

Sweet ones, know your Papa is good. You are no longer a slave in any way. He wants to continually throw a party in your honor not because you've done something right or because you have come home from the foreign land, but He wants to rejoice over you all the days of your life. Let Him be God. Let Him rejoice over His beautiful creation.

IDENTITY CRISIS

I didn't want to be just another orphan, Mr. Warbucks. I wanted to believe I was special.- Little Orphan Annie

IDENTITY CRISIS

5
ADOPTED

Once we are brought back into the family of God, we do so with full rites of the Kingdom. We aren't the little redheaded stepchild waiting for our Papa to finally come love on us. We are fully accepted from that moment on. It is a full blown party all of the time, a celebration of epic proportion because you are the relationship between you and Papa. There has never been a better Father, not Heathcliff Huxtable, Mike Brady, or Danny Tanner. His understanding far exceeds any sit down talk that Andy Taylor might have had with Opie. Whoever your dream parent might have been, you have already surpassed that when you were adopted by Papa.

What comes with this adoption? What are our rights as children of the Living God? Are we really co-heirs with Christ? What does that look like? Are we really part of the family? No matter what the relationship between you and your earthly parents looked like, it pales in comparison to being part of this family with Jesus as our brother and Papa as our Father.

Romans 8:14-17 NIV

¹⁴ For those who are led by the Spirit of God are the children of God. ¹⁵ The Spirit you received does not make you slaves, so that you live in fear again; rather, the Spirit you received brought about your adoption to sonship. And by him we cry, *"Abba,* Father." ¹⁶ The Spirit himself testifies with our spirit that we are God's children. ¹⁷ Now if we are children, then we are heirs—heirs of God and co-heirs with Christ, if indeed we share in his sufferings in order that we may also share in his glory.

We've talked a little about the things in these verses above. That we are no longer slaves, but that we are His children. What does co-heir really mean though?

Let's take it back to Jewish custom. The meaning of

"joint-heir" is very specific. It means heirs that receive identical inheritance. This means we have an exact share of everything that Jesus was given. Let that soak in. Everything Jesus was given.

So what was Jesus given? What can we expect to see? If we share in His sufferings, so that we can share in His glory. What is the glory? It's clear by that verse that we will inherit His sufferings, but we should see this nothing but joy. It is our honor to share in the sufferings of Christ.

2 Corinthians 1:4-6 NIV

4 who comforts us in all our affliction so that we will be able to comfort those who are in any affliction with the comfort with which we ourselves are comforted by God. For just as the sufferings of Christ are ours in abundance, so also our comfort is abundant through Christ. But if we are afflicted, it is for your comfort and salvation; or if we are comforted, it is for your comfort, which is effective in the patient enduring of the same sufferings which we also suffer.

Papa promised to comfort us while we go through these afflictions. It is in the comfort that we see the Glory. When the presence of God is so thick around you that it seems like you can reach out and take hold of it. That is some serious comfort.

I'm reminded of some of the things that Heidi Baker has talked about. She talks about being shot at, strangled, beaten up. She's not afraid.[ii] When you know that you are a joint-heir, that you are completely and lavishly loved by the Father, being afraid of someone else that God also loves, seems insignificant. Legions of angels are standing at the ready to come defend us, and yet our biggest defense is loving as Jesus loved. When you are a child of the King, whether you understand that yet or not, you respond to what is in your DNA. Our DNA is Love, because we are made in the image of our Papa. I have learned when I am approaching people on the street, no matter how afraid I am, if I come to them in Love, and in the authority of Jesus I have nothing to be afraid of.

Hebrews 13:6 NIV

So we say with confidence, "The Lord is my helper; I will not be afraid. What can mere mortals do to me?"

Even though we are facing death and persecution every day, we have nothing to fear. Our Lord is our helper. So we can step boldly into the mission field with confidence that our steps are being guided and ordered.

There are more scriptures on inheritance than I can reference in this book. From Genesis to Revelation, it is completely full of God speaking on the subject. It is an important topic for Him, something He takes so seriously that He is willing to give us not just a small portion but everything that He imparted to Jesus, lacking nothing.

What of the things that we saw Jesus do, are those part of our inheritance as well? I believe that the miracles of the Bible didn't pass away. I believe that all of the things that Jesus did, are still for us today. It is part of our inheritance. We are not without power, because we are filled with the Holy Spirit. It is not of our own strength but of God's that we can accomplish anything.

I believe walking and breathing is as much of a miracle as walking on water or making the dead breathe again. We can do nothing apart from our Father[18], but we can do all things through Him[19].

When I read the Gospel and I see the things that Jesus performed, I wonder why we don't see more of these things today. If we believe the scriptures, then we clearly know that we can do all that Jesus did. I think it's a matter of understanding our Identity. We aren't sure that those things are for us, so we don't act in faith that we can accomplish it. Jesus did only what the Father did.[20] Therefore anything that we do, we as children, do in Jesus name.

What if we were walking so clearly in our inheritance, our Identity that we could raise the dead? What if our understanding of being a joint-heir with Jesus was so palpable that we walked around and people were healed just by being in our presence? Think that's not possible? Take a look at this:

---

[18] John 15:5

[19] Philippians 4:13

[20] John 15:19

Acts 5:12-16 NIV

¹² The apostles performed many signs and wonders among the people. And all the believers used to meet together in Solomon's Colonnade. ¹³ No one else dared join them, even though they were highly regarded by the people. ¹⁴ Nevertheless, more and more men and women believed in the Lord and were added to their number. ¹⁵ As a result, people brought the sick into the streets and laid them on beds and mats so that at least Peter's shadow might fall on some of them as he passed by. ¹⁶ Crowds gathered also from the towns around Jerusalem, bringing their sick and those tormented by impure spirits, and all of them were healed.

Peter was walking in such authority of Jesus, that people were healed just by passing through Peter's shadow. We aren't talking about Jesus Himself. We are talking about Peter. The man who denied Jesus three times before the cock crowed.[21] What did Peter possess that we don't? That answer is easy. Relationship with Jesus. He was walking so close, so intimately with Jesus,

---
[21] Matthew 26:34

that healing became part of his everyday life.

Notice, Peter didn't try to heal. He didn't wave his hands over someone and fast for forty days straight. He went about his business and people were healed in his shadow. This is part of our inheritance. We have intimate access to Papa at all times. It is that intimacy that releases the Power of God, into the lives around us.

Think back through the Bible at all of the miracles that were performed. Old Testament and New Testament alike. What was so different back then, that they could do these things and we have the mindset that we can't. There is no difference, except we have a veil over our eyes. We are caught up in what we look like to the person sitting next to us in the pew. We don't want to look like the crazy, who is out preaching to the passing tourists on the streets. We don't put ourselves out there when we see a homeless vet that has lost his leg defending our country because we are afraid he might reject us. Or worse, that God wouldn't hear our cry for healing.

What happened to oil being filled to overflowing in once empty jars?[22] What about fire from heaven coming

---

[22] 2 Kings 4:5-7

down on to wet wood?[23] What of men who survived flames and came out not even smelling of smoke?[24] Walking on water[25], reattaching ears,[26] raising the dead[27].

John 14:12 NIV

"Truly, truly, I say to you, he who believes in Me, the works that I do, he will do also; and greater works than these he will do; because I go to the Father. Whatever you ask in My name, that will I do, so that the Father may be glorified in the Son"

Let me ask you this question. Did you ever see Jesus once not see complete healing when He prayed? Was there one time in the Bible that Papa said, *"Nope, not this time Jesus. They have been bad and probably should deal with that lost limb until they understand I'm a good and loving God."* If God heard and answered all of the prayers that Jesus prayed, and we have that co-heir inheritance, where is the breakdown? Why aren't we doing the same

---

[23] 1 Kings 18:37-39

[24] Daniel 3:26-27

[25] Matthew 14:22-23

[26] Luke 22:51

[27] John 11

thing like it says we can do in the Bible? The answer is our faith.

Deep down inside, we believe the lie that we are not one with Jesus. That we are not made in the image of God, that we are not fully adopted into the Kingdom.

Even the disciples had trouble fully understanding. Remember the demon they couldn't cast out?

Matthew 17:9 NIV

18 And Jesus rebuked him, and the demon came out of him, and the boy was cured at once. 19 Then the disciples came to Jesus privately and said, "Why could we not drive it out?" 20 And He said to them, "Because of the littleness of your faith; for truly I say to you, if you have faith the size of a mustard seed, you will say to this mountain, 'Move from here to there,' and it will move; and nothing will be impossible to you."

They weren't walking in their full identity as sons. If they had truly understood who they were, that their faith wasn't from them but from Jesus Himself, this boy would have been healed on the spot. I wonder how many miracles we miss out on seeing and performing because we don't lean on the faith of Jesus rather than our own.

Jesus wasn't saying that they must muster more faith, He was saying that the faith that they had wasn't from them in the first place. They were looking for the wrong faith. The only faith that has power is the one that comes from Jesus. He is the author and finisher of our faith. [28]

Our sonship, our adoption, is so much more important than we give it credence. We need to fully embrace who we are in the family of God.

---

[28] Hebrews 12:2

IDENTITY CRISIS

Once a man is broken, only love can pick up the pieces and glue him back together. - Unknown

6
GLUE

Did you know that there is a substance in your body that holds you together? Did you know that this substance is in the shape of a cross? It's called Laminin. I'm reminded of the verse in Colossians.

Colossians 1:15-20 NIV

[15] The Son is the image of the invisible God, the firstborn over all creation. [16] For in him all things were created: things in heaven and on earth, visible and

invisible, whether thrones or powers or rulers or authorities; all things have been created through him and for him. [17] He is before all things, and in him all things hold together. [18] And he is the head of the body, the church; he is the beginning and the firstborn from among the dead, so that in everything he might have the supremacy. [19] For God was pleased to have all his fullness dwell in him, [20] and through him to reconcile to himself all things, whether things on earth or things in heaven, by making peace through his blood, shed on the cross.

In Him, all things are held together. Some people try and say that Laminin is in the shape of a sword, or a caduceus. But, knowing that my Father created me, and knowing the importance of the cross before the foundation of the earth, I believe that it is a sign to us that He knows us so intimately that He even put the sign of the cross in the building blocks of our bodies.

Laminin is the glue of our bodies. It's a cell adhesion molecule. Without this in our bodies we would literally fall apart. It is what holds one membrane onto the next. There are many different types of Laminin performing different actions in our bodies. Have you ever stopped to think about the intricacies of our bodies? How complex and amazing the human machine is?

Louie Giglio is the one that first introduced me to Laminin.[29] I ran across his video on YouTube one day, and I haven't viewed how our bodies were created the same way since. If you haven't seen the video I encourage you to look it up. You can go to any medical book and pull up a picture of Laminin and it will look the same. This is not some Christian rendition of what they think that Laminin looks like. These images can be pulled from any science manual.

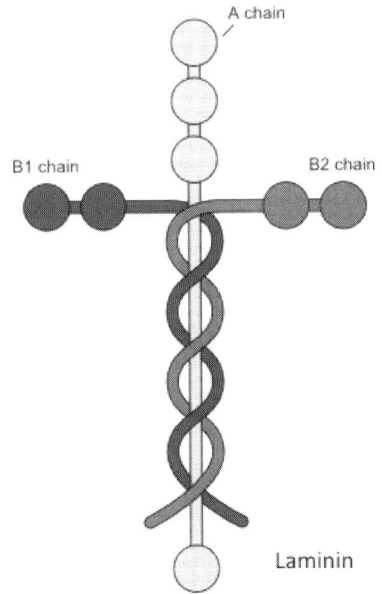

Notice there are three chains that make up Laminin. Something that I had never thought of before until I really started researching the subject. Not only is in the

---

[29] https://www.youtube.com/watch?v=iCrvibgo1LM

shape of the cross but its chains are woven together like a three strand cord. To me that is representative of the Trinity. We often use that verse in reference to our relationships. Us, the other person, and God. I also see that verse as the Holy Spirit, The Father, Jesus.

Ecclesiastes 4:12 NIV

Though one may be overpowered, two can defend themselves. A cord of three strands is not quickly broken.

I feel like we take the wonder of our bodies for granted a lot of the time. We don't take into consideration that our very breath is a miracle. We don't stop to think about our heart's function, how it beats night and day even when we are asleep.

DNA has always fascinated me. DNA is only made up of four chemicals. Much like a computer code of ones and zeroes, our DNA has a code made up of A,T,G, and C. Each tiny cell contains a code that is three billion letters long. It would take thirty one years, reading the code straight through day and night, to read it out loud from one cell.[30]

---

[30] Francis S. Collins, director of the Human Genome Project, *The Language of God*, (Free Press, New York, NY), 2006, p 1.

We don't realize that 99.9% of our DNA is similar to everyone else's. It is the tiny details, the tiny changes in that code, that make us unique. God is a God of unfathomable intricacy. Writing of that code was a unique, precise sequence that formed everything about you. We cannot explain away this beautiful language written in the very cells of our bodies. This language is what determines your hair color, eye color, the way you move and breathe. Every single bit of what makes you uniquely you is written in that language. God knew what sequence He would order in you before the earth was even created. It has been said that DNA is actually the blueprint for life.

There is beauty in the programming. Beauty in the thought that went into every single aspect of your life. Papa went into great detail to determine the exact shade of blue that your eyes turned out to be. A color that lights Him on fire when He looks deep into your eyes. The tone in your voice, the resonance when you sing, He created those things to please Himself.

Those things you might want to change about yourself, He created with purpose. The exact slope of your nose. The way your lips form that amazing smile in just a certain way. The strength in your hands, the gentleness in the graceful way that you walk. Your desire to dance, sing, even do math. He created you as a masterpiece. Your DNA is the blueprint. He is the architect. You are the building.

The Bible speaks about us being the temple of God. If we are His temple, don't you think that we would be marked somehow by His signature?

1 Corinthians 6:19-20 NIV

19 Or do you not know that your body is a temple of the Holy Spirit who is in you, whom you have from God, and that you are not your own? 20 For you have been bought with a price: therefore glorify God in your body.

You do know He thought about you when He created you, right? I will be honest. I still struggle with the knowledge that I was created for God to enjoy. I don't feel very enjoyable often. This past weekend I was able to go to a very special retreat. As I was talking to some of the ladies there, they kept coming up to me and telling me I was beautiful. It made me angry. I didn't want them to say these things. I broke down at one point and started talking about it to a friend of mine that was also there. I've been overweight for a long time. Sometimes I don't feel beautiful on the outside, but most of the time I am okay with how I look. Then I realized, I don't think I'm beautiful inside. The part of me that seeks God. The part of me that wants things, desires things. The deep down, the soul part of me felt ugly before God. When I realized this, it freed me a little.

As I went down to be alone by the lake that night, my head buried in the grass as I prayed. I was there at the foot of three crosses, and scenes of Jesus dying flooded my mind. He was fully man. That means that God knew what color eyes to give Him, what shade of hair he would have. The tiny details of His unique face. Jesus was all of those things that we are too. It humbled me. It broke me. It made me realize that the self-abuse that I had put myself through for those years had to stop because, I was one with God.

I'm pretty transparent about most things. But, there are a few deep-seeded insecurities that I rarely share with anyone. So here it goes.

I was just walking passed my bathroom mirror, tank top, underwear, hair a mess, no makeup on. I caught a glimpse of myself out of the corner of my eye. A glimpse of my body, and I thought to myself, *"It's not as horrible as I make it out to be."* It's actually not horrible at all. It's beautiful. God formed. I snapped a few photos of myself. I saw beauty in the flaw. I've had a rough couple of days accepting my worth as a woman. Even when you start to understand who you are in Christ, these days can come if you aren't constantly renewing your mind. Taking the photos made me appreciate the beauty of the machine that is my body. No, I don't look like a porn star, or even what the media thinks I should look like. I look like a real woman, with bumps and curves. I have scars and bruises. My hair is a glorious mess of curls, my face without wrinkle somehow. My heart is open and vulnerable to being rejected again, because when I love, I love with the fierceness of God. Fierceness is often rejected. I saw boldness in the mirror, a courageous woman. I saw a Proverbs 31 woman standing there, so in love with Jesus, her face was glowing. I saw a captivating beauty, captured in the awe of God's handiwork.

Psalms 139:13-15 NIV

13 For You formed my inward parts; You wove me in my mother's womb. 14 I will give thanks to You, for I am fearfully and wonderfully made; Wonderful are Your works, And my soul knows it very well. 15 My frame was not hidden from You, When I was made in secret, And skillfully wrought in the depths of the earth.

We are fearfully and wonderfully made. God knows every single working of not only our souls, but of our bodies. He made each chemical that forms your body.

Each element that is essential to human existence. The inner working of our hearts, pumping blood through an intricate highway of veins and capillaries. The way the trees give off oxygen that we involuntarily breathe in to fuel the cells that are held together by one cross shaped cell binding molecule. How can we look at these machines and say we aren't amazing?

How can we look at our human bodies, from the miraculous giving birth to our dying day and say there isn't a God who intellectually designed each aspect of our bodies, going further still knows each of us by name.

It says that He even knows the number of hairs on our heads. If He cares about such a tiny detail about our bodies, do you not think that He is madly in love with the creation that He made in you?

Luke 12:7 NIV

Indeed, the very hairs of your head are all numbered. Don't be afraid; you are worth more than many sparrows.

How beautiful we are to our Maker. How blessed we are to have such a thoughtful architect and builder. How blessed we are that He loves us with extravagancy shouting our worth to all of creation. It talks of how He knit us in our mother's womb. How He knew us before we were born.

Jeremiah 1:5 NIV

Before I formed you in the womb I knew you, before you were born I set you apart; I appointed you as a prophet to the nations.

Psalms 139:13 NIV

For you created my inmost being; you knit me together in my mother's womb.

Psalms 139:15-17 NIV

15 My frame was not hidden from You, When I was made in secret, And skillfully wrought in the depths of the earth; 16 Your eyes have seen my unformed substance; And in Your book were all written The days that were ordained for me, When as yet there was not one of them. 17 How precious also are Your thoughts to me, O God! How vast is the sum of them!

Job 31:15 ESV

Did not he who made me in the womb make him? And did not one fashion us in the womb?

Know, Beloved One, you are held together with the glue of God. You are a masterpiece created by the only Master who matters. You are loved.

Luke: I'm endangering the mission. I shouldn't have come.

Han Solo: It's your imagination, kid. Come on. Let's keep a little optimism here.

– Star Wars: Return of the Jedi

IDENTITY CRISIS

7
MIND CONTROL

One of the hardest things to get control of is our mind. I know that I flail and wrestle with what I know God is speaking to me and the circumstances that surround me. It often leads to confusion of great proportion and sometimes leaves me feeling like I can't hear Papa at all.

There are a few things in my life that I have been completely sure of, that I watched not happen. Yet, I know that I heard God correctly on them. These things will make a person lose their understanding of their Identity in Christ if we don't carefully and constantly tear down the vain imaginations of the world.

2 Corinthians 10: NIV

⁵ **We demolish arguments and every pretension that sets itself up against the knowledge of God, and we take captive every thought to make it obedient to Christ.**

So why didn't these precious things that I was believing for happen in the natural? Why did I believe for three years for something that just fell through my hands? I think the only answer here is that God can and will not force His will on us. He gave us free-will to move and live and act and breathe. Does it make God's Truth any less True? Absolutely not. His Truth remains even when we don't see the fruit of it.

I think of it like this- God's will is for all to come to knowledge of Christ. Yet, not all will choose to believe on His name, in Him, in the finished work of the Cross. It doesn't make His Truth and His promise any less real.

2 Peter 3:9 NIV

The Lord is not slack concerning his promise, as some men count slackness; but is longsuffering to us, not willing that any should perish, but that all should come to repentance

There are so many promises in the Bible that we can claim as our own, as well as promises that Papa gives us personally. One of the reasons we might not see these things come to fruition is our unbelief. It's hard to accept when we've been throwing ourselves into believing for something specific, whether it be a healing for a loved one or the long awaited child we've longed to hold in our arms. The truth is it never has been about our faith. We try and try to gain enough faith to see a miracle happen, but it's not about what we do. It's about Jesus' perfect faith, and our belief in Him.

When He is talking about the mustard seed, it's not about if we gain just enough of that faith, just that tiny bit of faith on our own. It's impossible to do. Jesus says in that scripture, *"Hey guys, you don't even have the faith of a tiny little mustard seed. Faith comes through me"*

Luke 17:6 NIV

He replied: "If you have faith as small as a mustard seed, you can say to this mulberry tree, 'Be uprooted and planted in the sea,' and it will obey you."

Matthew 17:20 NIV

He replied, "Because you have so little faith. Truly I tell you, if you have faith as small as a mustard seed, you can say to this mountain, 'Move from here to there,' and it will move. Nothing will be impossible for you."

Romans 10:17 NIV

¹⁷ Consequently, faith comes from hearing the message, and the message is heard through the word about Christ.

I was at an intensive grace school a few months back and the speaker was saying this very thing. That we are so lost without Jesus, that our faith isn't even our own. Even that comes through Him. He brought up the mustard seed illustration, and reminded us that we have often looked at that verse wrong. How many of us have used a little tiny mustard seed and gritted our teeth and clenched our fists and tried so hard to gather up the faith to move a mountain? I know I spent many years doing this, nights awake trying to gain just enough faith so that Papa would look on me with mercy and move that mountain to the sea.

I wish I had known the truth then. I wish I had been in a place where I could rely on Jesus alone to be my faith. Instead I felt inadequate because I could never quite have enough faith to have that mountain fall and crumble into the sea. I was still hurting and longing for more inside. I was still feeling defeated that even my faith wasn't enough.

Do you realize that your faith even for salvation isn't your own? That is even Jesus' faith. He imparts it to us as a gift. We have the choice to accept the gift or not.

Ephesians 2:8 NIV

For it is by grace you have been saved, through faith – and this not from yourselves, it is the gift of God

Some theologians say that it is the salvation that is the gift here. I agree. I also agree that it is the faith that is a gift. When we break it down to its simplest form we understand that we can do nothing. Let me repeat that- we can do *nothing* outside of Christ.

The break down happens when we think that we are in control. I'm a control freak. Giving up my imaginary control over my own universe is super scary to me. That's where the tearing down of strongholds enters into my life and I have to constantly focus on the Truths that God is the one in control.

Isaiah 45:6-7 ESV

That people may know, from the rising of the sun and from the west, that there is none besides me; I am the Lord, and there is no other. I form light and create darkness, I make well-being and create calamity, I am the Lord, who does all these things.

He is the one that sets the moon in place, tells the sun when to rise. He is the one that breathed life into every creature that has air in their lungs, yet we try and take control of our worlds. We act in vain.

I am preaching to the choir here. If there is any chapter that I've written that is for me, it's this one. I am the queen of trying to be in control of my situations. It doesn't usually work out in my favor.

I think because of my past experiences, I grasp for things that make me feel like I'm the one in control. For this reason, getting drunk or taking a bunch of drugs has never appealed to me. I need to be in control at all times. That is, until I met Holy Spirit.

I have learned that control is all an illusion. We weren't made to be in control. We were made to be loved on extravagantly by the Father. When those negative thoughts come into our head about our identity, we have to go to the scripture and seek out the truth about ourselves. Speak it out loud. There is power in the Word of God and there is power in the tongue.

Proverbs 18:21 NIV

The tongue has the power of life and death, and those who love it will eat its fruit.

I struggle with this so much. I have a thought come into my mind and instead of really seeking out the truth of it in the Scripture I automatically think the negative thought and give life to it. This is something Papa has been trying to teach me over the last year or so.

A few weeks ago, my friend and I were driving and I was attempting to give him directions. I was diagnosed as dyslexic and having dyscalculia in college. Because of this, it's hard for me to tell you my left from my right. I know which is which, but I have to think about it for a little bit sometimes. Often, I'm not fast enough when giving directions. I started to feel a little defeated in that moment, and I declared out.

"I'm just not good at directions. I don't know my left from my right and I'll never get it."

My friend looked at me and told me, in his famous words, *"Stop it."*

I stared at him for a minute, not knowing what to respond. He continued.

"When you say that you're giving life to it, stop it. Say you're good at giving directions"

"I'm great and fantastic at giving directions"

So now, when I catch myself complaining about how bad I am at giving directions, I change what I say. I speak life into myself. It's actually having an effect too, I'm more likely to tell you which direction is what. Our words are so powerful.

Our thoughts are so important too. It's been said many times that the battlefield of our spiritual lives is in our minds. If we go back to the garden, that is really what the fall was. Adam and Eve were suddenly aware of sin. Sin existed before, but upon eating of the fruit they became aware of it.

Genesis 3:5-7 NIV

"For God knows that in the day you eat from it your eyes will be opened, and you will be like God, knowing good and evil." 6 When the woman saw that the tree was good for food, and that it was a delight to the eyes, and that the tree was desirable to make one wise, she took from its fruit and ate; and she gave also to her husband with her, and he ate. 7 Then the eyes of both of them were opened, and they knew that they were naked; and they sewed fig leaves together and made themselves loin coverings.

Look at this. Their eyes were opened and they both knew they were naked. They were naked in the garden before and they never knew that there was anything wrong with their bodies. They suddenly had their eyes opened to sin- something God never created them to know.

Genesis 3:8-13 NIV

Then the man and his wife heard the sound of the LORD God as he was walking in the garden in the cool of the day, and they hid from the LORD God among the trees of the garden. ⁹But the LORD God called to the man, "Where are you?"

¹⁰He answered, "I heard you in the garden, and I was afraid because I was naked; so I hid."

¹¹And he said, "Who told you that you were naked? Have you eaten from the tree that I commanded you not to eat from?"

¹²The man said, "The woman you put here with me— she gave me some fruit from the tree, and I ate it."

¹³Then the LORD God said to the woman, "What is this you have done?"

The woman said, "The serpent deceived me, and I ate."

Pay close attention to this part. God went searching for them. It says Lord God. That would be Jesus. So Jesus is there, walking in the garden, looking for Adam. He is God, so He knows where Adam is, but still He calls for him. *Where are you?* He asks. Take this deep in your hearts Beloved. God went looking for man. Man in his sin did not go searching for God.

Adam answered, that he had heard God and he was afraid so he hid. How many times do we hide from God when we know we've screwed up? We stop going to church, we refuse to read our Bibles. We cover ourselves up with fig leaves of work and busyness, instead of laying it all out there naked before Papa.

God asks Adam, *Who told you that you were naked?* That question is profound. They had to be told, they had to believe the lie. Eve shouldn't have even known what deception was. She was to live a life being fully present in the garden with her Maker. She was to live a life of pure ecstasy in being one with God. She was never made to endure hard labor, painful child birth, death.

Because of the Blood of Jesus, we can go back to that garden. Our minds have been reset. We are covered in radical grace. All we have to do is speak the truth of who we are. Who Papa made us to be. In that truth of our Identity, we see glimpses of our real selves. The one that was never meant to leave the garden for a moment. We live in expectation of the miraculous, because that is what comes natural in the Kingdom.

When those thoughts come in, try to invade what you know to be the truth about yourself, who God created you to be, speak forth the truth of who God says you are. Whose God says you are. You don't belong to this world, but you are a new creation in Jesus Christ.

2 Corinthians 5:17-21 NKJV

17 Therefore, if anyone *is* in Christ, *he is* a new creation; old things have passed away; behold, all things have become new. 18 Now all things *are* of God, who has reconciled us to Himself through Jesus Christ, and has given us the ministry of reconciliation, 19 that is, that God was in Christ reconciling the world to Himself, not imputing their trespasses to them, and has committed to us the word of reconciliation.

20 Now then, we are ambassadors for Christ, as though God were pleading through us: we implore *you* on Christ's behalf, be reconciled to God. 21 For He made Him who knew no sin *to be* sin for us, that we might become the righteousness of God in Him.

1 LAW BREAKER

Are You a Law-Breaker?

DAY ONE
Breaking the Law

DAY TWO
Rest

DAY THREE
Letting Go of Religious Laws

DAY FOUR
What Has You in Bondage?

DAY FIVE
Relationship vs Law

DAY TWO

Exodus 20:8-10, NIV

Remember the Sabbath day by keeping it holy. [9] Six days you shall labor and do all your work, [10] but the seventh day is a Sabbath to the LORD your God. On it you shall not do any work, neither you, nor your son or daughter, nor your male or female servant, nor your animals, nor any foreigner residing in your towns. [11] For in six days the LORD made the heavens and the earth, the sea, and all that is in them, but he rested on the seventh day. Therefore the LORD blessed the Sabbath day and made it holy.

Papa gave us the Sabbath for a reason. He knows we need rest. We were not made to keep going non-stop. Yet we go and we go. Taking the kids to all of their after school activities. Being involved in every single ministry at the church. Taking on more than one Bible study.

The Jews in Jesus time made it more work than rest. Papa calls us to rest in Him, in all things.

Questions

1. In Exodus 20, the Bible talks about God giving us the day of rest. Even God Himself took a day of rest. How do you take a day of rest? What does it look like to you?

   _____
   _____
   _____
   _____

2. Why do you think that God took a day off after He was finished creating?

   _____
   _____
   _____

3. In your own words, what does worship mean?

   _____
   _____
   _____

4. Name three things that you struggle with that you need to find the rest of God in.

   _____
   _____
   _____

5. What are your favorite Bible verses regarding rest?

   _____

4. Is there any adversity in your life that you attribute to God punishing you instead of it just being circumstance? List them. Ask God to take the guilt that you feel from you. There is freedom in Christ.

_____
_____
_____
_____
_____
_____
_____

DAY FIVE

Good relationships don't punish. Good relationships don't hold things over the others head, expecting them to meet requirements in order to be loved. Our Papa doesn't do this either. We are not bound by law, but by relationship. When we do something, we do it not for fear of being punished, but out of love.

1. List your favorite scriptures talking about God's love for you.

_____
_____
_____
_____

2. What can you do that will strengthen your relationship with Papa?

   _____
   _____
   _____
   _____
   _____

3. In your own words, explain the difference between strictly following the law vs having a true relationship with Papa.

   _____
   _____
   _____
   _____

JOURNAL

_____
_____
_____
_____
_____
_____
_____
_____
_____
_____
_____

JENNIFER TODD-FLORA

IDENTITY CRISIS- JOURNAL

_____
_____

DAY FOUR

Read Isaiah 61. Jesus has come to set you free from any bondage, even that which is self-imposed. Search your heart over what you have learned and read this week. Ask Papa to reveal in you any areas that you are not in complete freedom to God's love for you.

1. Where do you struggle to be free?
   _____
   _____

2. How can resting in Papa's love for you bring you freedom?
   _____
   _____
   _____
   _____

3. List three of your favorite scriptures that speak of God's freedom for us.
   _____
   _____
   _____

DAY THREE

We say we don't believe in works, but how many of us feel like we have to uphold certain things that are expected of us? Let's burn the sacred cows that have no bearing on our goodness, or even more importantly, God's love of us.

1. Do you believe you have to perform in order for Papa to love you?

2. What sacred cows do you have in your life that are hard to let go of?

3. What do you think God wants of you rather than works?

IDENTITY CRISIS- JOURNAL

Questions

1. What had traditions been elevated to?
   Created into laws to make others feel inferior

2. Do you feel that you have to do certain things in order to get God's attention or love?
   sometimes. I don't always feel like a "good" christian

3. Imagine yourself as Mary, learning that Jesus was teaching in the Temple, how do you think you would have reacted?

4. Why do you think that the law was that you couldn't even spit on the Sabbath?
   it seems like any human act was considered work and dishonor to God

5. What Religious Laws do you enforce on yourself?
   I try to enforce the sabath to an extent

6. What can you do to break yourself of these mindsets?

My sweet-ones, I am so thankful that you have made the choice to uncover your true Identity. This journey may be tough for some of you, easier for others. If you take it to heart, it will be one of the most rewarding things you can ever do for yourself. Your relationship with Papa will strengthen, will deepen. You will find a place of rest that can only be found in God.

You will learn to love yourself, see yourself as Papa sees you. You will see that you are the spitting image of your Good Father. You will understand that you are good, loving, kind, and when you understand that, it will flow over to the others in your everyday life.

Enjoy this journey beautiful loved creatures. Be raw and open with yourselves. Take your time.

DAY ONE

Were you shocked to know how many laws Jesus broke? I know we view Jesus as this honey-haired blue-eyed man that hangs on our wall in Sunday School. The real Jesus is far from that sweet image. He is fully God, and fully man. He is sarcastic, tough, and loving all at the same time.

It's been said that Jesus taught "Grace on Steroids". He was making the point that there is no way we can ever fulfill the law, yet even today we feel like we have to do certain things to make Papa look in our direction. We believe if we pray a certain way then maybe He will answer us. When all He wants from us, is us.

IDENTITY CRISIS
Finding Your In Christ
STUDY GUIDE AND JOURNAL

JENNIFER TODD-FLORA

Pippin: I didn't think it would end this way.

Gandalf: End? No, the journey doesn't end here. Death is just another path… One that we all must take. The grey rain-curtain of this world rolls back, and all turns to silver glass… And then you see it.

Pippin: What? Gandalf?… See what?

Gandalf: White shores… and beyond, a far green country under a swift sunrise.

Pippin: Well, that isn't so bad.

-Lord of the Rings

IDENTITY CRISIS

8
FINISHED

"It is finished." Possibly some of the most important words ever written. When Jesus spoke out those words He declared over us for all time that everything that was set in motion from the foundation of the earth was now complete. His hard service was done. We were back in full communion with our Father if we just accepted His free gift of adoption.

When He declared it finished, He declared a beginning for us. Swooping us up in the arms of Grace and placing us in the throne room with our Father. No more roaming the streets looking for a home. We were now restored back to our Father who loves us enough to send His son, fully God, to become humanity on our behalf.

John 19:30 NIV

When he had received the drink, Jesus said, "It is finished." With that, he bowed his head and gave up his spirit.

We've talked about who Jesus was, how He broke the mosaic law, while keeping the Father's law. We've talked about being the mirror image of God, and how we died with Him on the cross. We've even talked about the beauty in the science regarding how the machines that are our bodies function. We have talked about tearing down the strongholds in our mind that come against our Identity in Christ, but now we've come to the most important part of our Identity. What happened on the cross that Friday afternoon.

Let's go over the events leading up to it. Jesus celebrated Passover with his friends. Giving them the commandment to remember Him when they eat of the bread and drink of the vine.[31]

He went to the garden of Gethsemane. Gethsemane actually means *"oil press"*. Jesus agonizes over what is about to take place, but ultimately prays *"not my will but thine."* [32]

He is betrayed by Judas and arrested in the early morning hours.[33] He was brought before Pilate,[34] then sent to Herod[35] and back to Pilate.[36] This all took place in very early morning, most likely before six a.m. Many scholars think that Pilate didn't think Jesus would be crucified, but gave in because of the screaming crowd. [37]

---

[31] Matthew 26:20-30; Mark 14:17-26; Luke 22:14-38; John 13:21-30

[32] Matthew 26:36-46; Mark 14:32-42; Luke 22:39-45

[33] Matthew 26:47-56; Mark 14:43-52; Luke 22:47-53; John 18:1-11

[34] Matthew 27:11-14; Mark 15:2-5; Luke 23:1-5; John 18:28-37

[35] Luke 23:6-12

[36] Luke 23:11

[37] Matthew 27:26; Mark 15:15; Luke 23:23-24; John 19:16

There were many illegal things pertaining to Jesus' sentence. A trial should have only taken place in the meeting places of the Sanhedrin. It shouldn't take place on the eve of a Sabbath or a Feast day, and never at night. A sentence of guilty was only to be given the day after a trial, not right away as in the case of Jesus.

I won't get into all of the laws broken that night, it's a book in itself, but there were many. The injustice that was handed to Him was great, and yet He took it with determination. He took it with you on His mind.

During His beating His hands would have been tied to a post while soldiers took a weapon they called a flagrum and used it to tear into His flesh. This instrument would have had many pieces of leather on it with each one consisting of bits of bone and metal tied to the ends. By Jewish law it says that Jesus would have received 39 blows to His back, although the exact number wasn't recorded in the Bible. They weren't known for following the law that day, so the exact number that Jesus received is not known.

When Jesus was struck, the bits of bone would tear into His flesh, ripping it open. The pieces of metal, probably in the form of a heavy ball, would bruise the flesh and tear it open at the same time. The first few strikes would have left large bruises and tears into the skin. The blows that would come after would have ripped into the muscles themselves, riddling them like shredded paper. The metal still bruising with every hit. The blood loss from this alone would have been great, and more excruciating that we can possibly imagine.

After the beating, He was stripped of His clothes, spit on, mocked, made to wear a robe and a crown of thorns.[38] The thorns were thick and long, pressed into his scalp with such force that the blood ran down his face and into His eyes making it next to impossible to see. Each one of the thorns was most likely one to two inches long and instead of being the traditional ring or circle, it covered his entire head. The soldiers continued beating Him, driving the long thorns deep into his scalp. The robe He was forced to wear was most likely that of a Roman Officer, purple or scarlet in color. The significance of the crown and robe, are defined with the thorns appearing on the earth only after the fall and the color of scarlet being a symbol of sin. This signifies that He took on the curse

---

[38] Matt 27:31

and the sin of men. His beard would have been plucked out as talked about in **Isaiah 50:6**, although it is not recorded in the gospels. The robe that was stuck to the drying sticky blood on His back was ripped off abruptly exposing the torn flesh to the elements again, causing it to bleed profusely.

After the beating He had to walk the Via Dolorosa, which means *"the way of suffering."* It was around 650 yards, or the length of six and a half football fields. He had to carry the cross bar of His cross on his back. It weighed between 80 and 110 pounds. He was already exhausted from being awake all night, sweating blood in the garden because of the extreme stress, being beaten nearly to death. When He fell underneath the weight of the beam, it was likely that the crushing weight caused a contusion in His heart. Simon of Cyrene was asked to carry His cross the rest of the way.

Once at the site of the crucifixion, the patibulum, or the cross bar would have been laid on the ground. Jesus would have been laid on top of this with His arms outstretched to each side. Square nails that were around 7 inches long were then driven into the wrists around the median nerve. This would have caused shocks of pain to radiate through both arms.

The posts at the crucifixion site would have been already standing and approximately 7 feet tall. These posts were called stipes. In the center of the stipe there would have been a crude made seat to support the victim.

The patibulum was then lifted on to the stipe and the knees of Jesus would have been bent and rotated laterally, in a very uncomfortable position. Then His feet would have been nailed to the stipe, once again using the same 7 inch nails.

Hanging in this position on the cross, it made it impossible to exhale and difficult to take in a full breath. Because of lack of oxygen and loss of blood there would be even more severe cramping in the muscles.

While Jesus was suffering this horrific painful death, He was also taking on all of man's humanity. All of the doubt that we have about God loving us, the abandonment we feel, the separation we feel from Papa. He took on the full range of our emotions and feelings. He finally cries out. About the ninth hour Jesus cried out in a loud voice, *"Eloi, Eloi, lama sabachthani--which means, My God, my God, why have you forsaken me?"*[39]

Jesus would die a slow suffocating death. Small areas of His lungs would start to collapse. Decreased oxygen would mean increased carbon dioxide, leading to acid build up in the muscles. Fluid would start to build up in His lungs. His heart would begin to fail.

He was offered two drinks. One was a spiced wine. In Biblical times spiced wine was often laced with opium. Jesus refused the spiced wine, going into this with a clear head and taking on all of the pain. He takes a drink of wine vinegar, which would have been made from fermented grapes and yeast. Yeast is a symbol of sin. He would drink it from a hyssop, also symbolic. The hyssop was used to apply the blood over the doors during The Passover.

Note that Jesus didn't give up His life because He was forced to, He gives it up on His own free-will. Like the free-will that the Father gives us today.

John 10:17-18 NIV

---

[39] Matthew 27:46:

"The reason my Father loves me is that I lay down my life--only to take it up again. No one takes it from me, but I lay it down on my own accord. I have authority to lay it down and authority to take it up again. This command I received from my Father."

Let it be noted, Jesus chose when to die. His life was not taken from Him, but He laid it down at the time that He decided to. Death by crucifixion could last up to nine days. Jesus was only on the cross a few hours. He had power over death, when He laid down His life and also when He was resurrected.

John 19:30 NIV

29A jar full of sour wine was standing there; so they put a sponge full of the sour wine upon a branch of hyssop and brought it up to His mouth. 30Therefore when Jesus had received the sour wine, He said, "It is finished!" And He bowed His head and gave up His spirit.

It is finished. With those words, came our Identity, restored back to us in its fullness. No longer are we lost without eyes to see, no longer are we orphans, no longer are we sentenced to death. It is finished, and we are whisked back to the garden. Fully alive, God fully alive in us. He is closer than the air we breathe, more real than anything we can touch, taste, or feel.

We are His beloved children, and our love story with Him, is the greatest one ever told. More romantic than any movie, any great wartime tale. This is who you are. This is what He died to give you back. This is who you were always created to be and will forever be. You are His, and He is yours ending your Identity Crisis forever. Your Identity is Christ, when you understand and believe in what He has done for you, you are no longer your own, You have the King of Kings living inside of you. Welcome to your new Identity in Christ.

I AM

A child of God - Romans 8:16

Redeemed from the Hand of the Enemy - Psalm 107:2

Forgiven - Colossians 1:13-14

Saved by Grace Through Faith - Ephesians 2:8

Justified - Romans 5:1

Sanctified - 1 Corinthians 1:2

A New Creature - 2 Corinthians 5:17

Partaker of His Divine Nature - 2 Peter 1:4

Redeemed from the Curse of the Law - Galatians 3:13

Delivered from the Powers of Darkness - Colossians 1:13

Led by the Spirit of God - Romans 8:14

A Son or Daughter of God - Romans 8:14

Kept in Safety Wherever I Go - Psalms 91:11

Getting All of My Needs Meet - Philippians 4:19

Casting All My Cares on Jesus - 1 Peter 5:7

Strong in the Lord and in the Power of His Might - Ephesians 6:10

Doing All Things Through Christ - Philippians 4:13

An Heir of God and Joint Heir with Jesus - Romans 8:17

Heir to the Blessing of Abraham - Galatians 3:26

Blessed Coming in and Going Out - Deuteronomy 28:13

Heir of Eternal Life - 1 John 5:11-12

Blessed with Blessings - Ephesians 1:3

Healed - 1 Peter 2:24

Conqueror - Romans 8:37

Overcomer- Revelation 12:11

Righteousness of God in Christ- 2 Corinthians 5:21

Imitator of Jesus- Ephesians 5:1

Light of the World- Matthew 5:14

ABOUT THE AUTHOR

Jennifer was born and raised in Arkansas, where she came to know Jesus at an early age. At fourteen she discovered her calling to ministry and mission work while on a youth trip to Mexico with her church.

In 2008, after a life-altering experience with the Holy Spirit, Jennifer began her work in women's and marriage ministry serving people all over the globe. In 2013, she received her minister's license and moved to the Dallas, Texas area to work with the homeless, bringing the Love of Jesus to those on the streets.

She is also the founder of Not The End, a suicide and self-harm prevention foundation. She speaks to youth groups and parents alike, sharing that there is hope for those who have been in the depths of depression and self-harm.

It is her deep passion to share the Love of Jesus with others, to teach that our God is a good and loving Father and that the Holy Spirit is alive and moving in our lives today. Jennifer teaches the finished work of the Cross and believes that every person is reachable by sharing the Good News by loving as Jesus loves.

Jennifer currently resides in Arlington, Texas with her two year old Yorkie, Lydia. She continues to work with Not The End, as well as her new ministry Zion's Strength.

FOR BOOKING INFORMATION

Please write to us at:

zionsstrength@gmail.com

www.zionsstrength.com
www.nottheend.com

find us on Facebook:

Not The End or
Zion's Strength

[i] Mackenzie, Ian K. (February 2004). "The Stockholm Syndrome Revisited: Hostages, Relationships, Prediction, Control and Psychological Science". *Journal of Police Crisis Negotiations*

[ii] Baker, Heidi (February 2014). "Finding Your Power in God's Lavish Love" Charisma Magazine

Made in the USA
San Bernardino, CA
30 August 2014